The new bible for Kitchen simpletons

"I thought this book was going to be shit, but actually, it's not quite that bad." Grenville, one of Graham's friends.

"This book is the perfect gift for someone who needs to buy a gift…" The owner of a giftshop somewhere.

Other books by Graham Hey:

Confessions of an Invisible Man. A rom-com about a kitchen porter called Cooper McCrae who is going to be invisible for exactly seven days. This is actually brilliant. Published by Chronos Publishing.

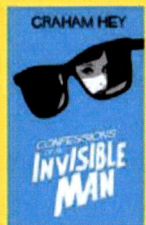

Let's Hear it for the Boy. A rom-com set in the 1980's. It's hilarious according to spoon bender Uri Geller - and we didn't even pay him to say that. Published by Chronos Publishing.

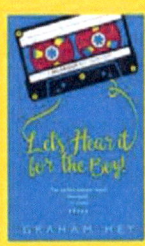

Coming Soon: To Be Tendulkar - another romantic comedy - this time set in Leeds. Rav Bhutta is about to get a single wish. Will he fuck up? Probably.

Credits

Thanks to: Chloe Hopper, Vicky Wong, Matt Whetstone and Nigel Fitzhenry for their recipe contributions and ideas. Thanks also to janespattisserie.com for inspiring me to do more in the kitchen, and natashaskitchen.com and insanelygoodrecipes.com. Also, thanks to Julie, my wife, who has hardly seen me recently as I've been locked away writing this. Mind you, she's happy enough watching Corrie and Emmerdale.

As usual, a huge thank you to Taryn Johnston of Chronos Publishing for encouraging me to do this book. It has taken me longer than expected, but I've also been trying to write my next novel at the same time. Anyway, thanks Taryn – you're the best!

The author with his taste tester

A final word from the author...

Well, that's just about it for now. I hope you've enjoyed my little ideas combined with gratuitous swearing. Please try a few of these things, as I think you may well adopt them into your own culinary repertoire.

If you do try any of these, then be sure to message me via social media and tell me what a success your meal turned out to be. Please do not send me any penis photos.

So, a big thank you for actually getting this far (unless you've just flipped straight to the back), I do appreciate it. It's now time for me to go, as I have a court appearance in the morning, and I need an early night.

Good night and God bless.

Notes

This cake will last at room temperature for about 3 or 4 days. Don't stick it in the fridge or it will dry out very quickly and be shite.

I use a cake tin to store it in – I got it for Christmas.

You can use dark chocolate in place of the cocoa powder if you wish - use 100g for the sponge, and 100g for the buttercream.

If your cake isn't baked fully, your oven might be at the wrong temperature, or it wasn't mixed correctly. Keep it in the oven until a skewer comes out clean, and it's springy to touch. Once your cake has been in the oven for about 30 minutes it's OK if you open the door to keep testing it with a knife or skewer. It'll be fine.

Q&A Quickies

*Questions sent in by members of the public via the internet.

Q: How big should a slice of cake be?
A: According to industry insiders, a slice of cake should be big enough so that when you have it handed to you on a plate you don't immediately think 'the stingy twat has only given me a tiny piece!'

Q: I don't have a cake tin to put it in like yours. Once I've baked my cake, is it acceptable to put it into my motorbike helmet with some Cling film over the top?
A: Only an absolute cretin would consider doing that. So, in your case, I'd say that's fine.

Q: Can you microwave chocolate to warm it up?
A: Yes, you can.

*This is a variation of a cake I originally saw on janespattiserie.com which is a brilliant blog/website.

Chocolate Cake for Dummies

This dead easy chocolate cake should take you about ten minutes to prepare, fifteen minutes if you're a moron. Twenty minutes if you're a student. This is a delicious chocolate cake and I swear that once you've tasted it, you'll want to bake it again.

Sometimes, I think there is too much filling in cakes, when the best bit is the sponge of the cake itself so I've halved the usual ingredients for the butter cream, but there's still plenty in there so you can taste it alright.

Chocolate Cake ingredients

- 250g of Unsalted Butter
- 250g Caster Sugar
- 245g Self Raising Flour
- 55g Cocoa Powder
- 6 Medium Eggs

Chocolate Buttercream filling

- 100g Unsalted Butter
- 200g Icing Sugar
- 25g Cocoa Powder
- You'll also need a couple of Cadbury's milk chocolate bars and a couple of twirls.

This is what you need to do...

1. Don't get cold feet at this stage - you won't regret it. Firstly, preheat your oven to 180C. (160C if you've got a fan oven).
2. Now, you'll need to line two 8-inch cake tins with greaseproof paper. This is a right pain to do, but if you don't do it, your cake will stick to the tins. Basically, you'll be fucked.
3. Mix your butter and sugar together. I use a fork for this. And keep doing it until it's fluffy. Then add the flour, eggs and cocoa powder and stir it in until it's really well mixed and smooth.
4. Once it's all nicely mixed, pour half into each cake tin. Put about the same amount of mixture into each tin and then bake in the oven for about 30 minutes. It can take a bit longer so keep your eye on things. At 30 minutes, open the oven and stick a sharp knife or skewer into the cake so see if it's done. When you remove the knife, have a look at the blade, and if it's clean, then your cake is done. If there's some of the cake mix stuck to the blade, give it a few more minutes.
5. Once it's done, leave it to cool for about ten minutes or so and then stick it on to a wire rack until it's properly cooled.

For the Chocolate Buttercream that's the bit in the middle...

1. Always use butter for this, do not use any of that fake butter. I've used that fake stuff now and again when I've run out of proper butter, and it's never as good. Although it's not shit, either to be fair.
2. Beat the butter on its own for a minute to get it nice and loose. Add the icing sugar slowly and mix it all up a bit at a time. Just don't add it all at once. Then add the Cocoa Powder and mix it all together.
3. If it's really very stiff, add in ONE tablespoon of boiling water at a time, beating fully each time, until it becomes smooth and lovely.

To Decorate

1. Place your first sponge on a cutting board and spread on half of the buttercream. Now put the other cake on top of this.
2. Now melt the Cadbury's chocolate bar/s in the microwave and when it's all runny, pour it all over the top of your cake. I use a knife to spread it about a bit. Then I break up some Twirls (or Flakes) and place the bits into the melted chocolate. You can also add some sprinkles if you want. The last time I made a chocolate cake, I melted a Terry's Chocolate Orange and poured that over the top. It was delicious.

A Doddle of a Banana Cake

Someone once asked me, "Do you actually need bananas to make a banana cake?" I said, "Of course you fucking do, or it wouldn't be called a banana cake, would it? Jesus Christ, some people are so thick.

Ingredients

- 3 very ripe medium bananas
- 3 large eggs. Use free-range eggs if you can afford. *A free-range egg is supposed to be an egg where the chickens roam around the field to their hearts content. Cute. However, what it really means is that there are about a million chickens running wild and free within a 3-metre square space.
- 100g soft light brown sugar
- 150ml sunflower or vegetable oil
- 275g white self-raising flour
- 1 tsp ground mixed spice (is this really necessary? Probably not!)
- 1 tsp baking powder

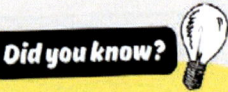

Steamed banana cake is found in Chinese, Malaysian, Indonesian and Vietnamese cuisine according to Wikipedia, but I've also seen it online where they say it was invented in America. That's typical, that is – the Yanks trying to take credit for it. Next, they'll be taking credit for McDonalds!

Method

1. Preheat the oven to 180C/160C Fan/Gas 4 and grease and line a 900g/2lb loaf tin with baking parchment or use a loaf tin liner. It's a bit of a faff, but you should really try and do this.
2. Peel the bananas and mash with a fork. Tip into a large mixing bowl and add the eggs, sugar and oil. Use a fork or whisk to mix it all together.
3. Add the flour, spice (if you can be arsed) and baking powder and whisk together until thoroughly mixed-up. Pour into the tin. Bake for 40 minutes, or until the cake is well risen and a skewer inserted into the middle comes out clean. Have you ever done that before? If you don't have a skewer handy – and why the fuck would you – just stick the blade of a knife in. If you're in a street gang, you probably already carry a blade, so you can use this.
4. Cool in the tin for 10 minutes, then tip it out onto a wire rack. One of those racks out of the oven will do.
5. Proceed to eat.

Banana cake is good with:

A bit of butter on, says my next-door neighbour. But I told her to mind her own fucking business.
A cup of tea.

To enhance your banana cake experience, why not to listen to some music. I find that The Lathums or The Killers do the job.

Preparation time: Not long really.

Rice Pudding

I can already feel that some of you are already about to skip this page. But don't! Rice pudding done well is one of the greatest things ever invented. Please try this, and then make your mind up. Honestly, you really need to have a go at this.

This is a slight variation of a recipe I used from an old Delia Smith book and it's brilliant. And, it's surprisingly easy to make.

Tell me how to make it then!
OK, hold your horses.

This is what you'll need:

- Pudding rice (175ml level in a measuring jug. That's probably about 17,467 individual rice grains, but who's going to count them? Not me.
- 400g of evaporated milk
- 850g of whole milk
- 25 g real butter
- 35g of granulated sugar
- 1 nutmeg
- You'll need an ovenproof dish to out your rice pudding in, and also an oven. If you don't have an oven, then forget it.

OK, let's do this!

1. Butter your ovenproof dish. That means rub some butter all around the base and the edges.
2. Now turn on your oven to 150 degrees C. Fan ovens 130.
3. Now put the rice and the sugar in the ovenproof dish along with the milk and stir it all up.
4. Pick up your nutmeg and use a grater to sprinkle it all over the top. Use all the nutmeg. Finally, finish off by putting the butter on top break it into very little pieces and dot it about a bit. That was piss easy.
5. Now put it into the oven. Be careful or it will all slosh about and spill over the floor. Leave it in the oven for about 2 hours and fifteen minutes. When it's done, it will have a lovely brown skin over the top of it and the rice will be super soft. Test it to see if it's done.
6. I think the skin is the best part of it. If you've never tasted it, give it a go.

Serving suggestion: Eat with a spoon

True story...

I made this rice pudding to cheer myself up recently. I went to see a Bee Gees tribute act, but it was cancelled at the last minute. Tragedy.

Rocky Road with Biscoff!

Here's a great recipe for rocky road – and I think you'll make it again and again because it's so good! This is a variation of a recipe I found online and it's fair to say that the people who I tested it on ate it like gannets. There was hardly a piece left for me, the selfish twats. Anyhow, at least they liked it.

The great thing about this recipe is that there's no cooking involved at all. That's a bit like magic isn't it?

Ingredients

- 350g White Chocolate buttons or chocolate bars.
- 50g Unsalted Butter
- 125g Biscoff Spread (or the fake Biscoff Spread will also do the trick)
- 150g Mini Marshmallows (large marshmallows are also perfect for this!)
- 250g Biscoff Biscuits (you can use those unbranded 'Biscoff-style' biscuits you can get in Aldi. I've used those and you can't tell the difference...)

Music

When I'm making this recipe, I like to listen to XTC, the new wave band from the early 1980's. When doing so, my Rocky Road always seems to turn out much better. All together now... 1,2,3,4,5... Senses Working Over-time etc.

Things to do whilst eating your Rocky Road

- Watch a crime drama on the telly
- Tickle your cat. On second thoughts, don't do this as it's unhygienic if you're eating...
- Read a book. Perhaps 'Confessions of an Invisible Man' by me. And then put a great review of it online!

Instructions

1. Get a 9-inch square tin and put some parchment paper in it. If you don't know what parchment paper is, just google it for fuck's sake. It's basically greaseproof paper and you can get it in any supermarket.
2. Get a large glass bowl and add the chocolate and the butter. Now put some water in a larger pan and place the bowl with the chocolate in, into the pan. And put the pan on the cooker and turn it on. Use a low heat until all the butter and chocolate melts. If this sounds too complicated, just add the butter and chocolate into a bowl and microwave it for 20 seconds at a time and keep stirring it until it's all melted.
3. Melt the Biscoff Spread by shoving it into a microwave until it's all runny. Then tip this into the melted chocolate/butter that you did a minute ago.
4. At this point you're not far off finished. Pretty easy, eh? Now add in all the Marshmallows and all the broken biscuits and mix it all together. Once it's well mixed, pour it all into the tin you prepared earlier and spread it around so it's all nice and even.

Stick it into the fridge until it's all set. If you think you've made too much you can do one of two things. 1. Just eat more of it. Or 2. Next time you make it, you can half all the quantities and it will make half as much. Even NASA will tell you it's not rocket science! This will last for up to seven days in your fridge, but you can bet it will be eaten long before then.

Sticky Toffee Pudding

Sticky toffee pudding is the thing I always choose when I see it on a menu anywhere.

Normally, I wouldn't recommend you make your own sticky toffee pudding – especially when the supermarket ones are great and only cost two or three quid a pop. However, if you fancy actually trying to make a pudding, then this is a great one to try. I've kept it as simple as possible, so anyone should be able to make it. Honestly, this is a very basic way to make an award-winning pud.

Ingredients

- 75g unsalted butter
- 1 tsp bicarbonate of soda
- 165g light or dark brown soft sugar
- 250g self raising flour
- 3 medium-sized eggs
- 1 tsp baking powder
- 65g golden syrup
- 250ml whole milk. Don't use that semi-skimmed stuff for this.

Instructions for the Pudding

1. Preheat your oven to 180ºC/160ºC Fan and get a baking dish ready I use one that is about 30x20cm-ish.
2. Add the unsalted butter, sugar, eggs, self-rising flour, baking powder, bicarbonate of soda, and the black treacle into a bowl, and mix it all together until it's all mixed up. Don't mix it together for too long, just a minute or so will be enough.
3. Pour over the milk and leave the mixture to sit for about a quarter of an hour. You can use a blender on the mixture if you think it's a bit too lumpy. Mix it until it's smooth if it makes you happy. If you've been told you're not allowed near electric gadgets, then ask a responsible adult to help you.
4. Add in the milk a bit at a time, and then mix it until it's smooth. The mixture might look very runny, but leave it, it's supposed to look like that.
5. Now pour the mixture into the dish and bake in the oven for 35-40 minutes, or until a skewer comes out clean. While your sticky toffee pudding is cooking, you might as well make yourself useful and make the sauce. Of course, if you really cannot be arsed to make a sauce, you can always buy one from your favourite supermarket. These sauces are usually in the baking section, which is usually near the bread.

Did you know?
I've been told that sticky toffee pudding was invented somewhere in the Lake District. That sort of makes sense cos they've got fuck all else to do up there apart from complain about hikers leaving gates open.

OK, here's the recipe you need for the toffee sauce.

- 65g unsalted butter
- 2 tbsp of golden syrup
- 1 tsp vanilla extract
- 140 ml double cream
- 75g light or dark brown soft sugar

1. Put all the ingredients into a large pan, heat it and stir until the butter has melted and the sugar has dissolved. Keep the sauce on the heat until it boils and stir for a couple of minutes, so it starts to thicken up a bit. Pour about half of the sauce over the baked pud.
2. How you serve your sticky toffee pudding is up to you. Many people like ice cream with it, some prefer custard and yet others prefer cream with it. What a complex world we live in. We do though, don't we?

Note: The sauce will last for about three days in the fridge.

Easy Ice Cream Pudding

This is so easy. There's no cooking or any of that crap to do.

What do you need?
- Ice cream (Tesco soft scoop)
- 2 x Twix
- Maple syrup
- A flake

Now do this...
Scoop some ice cream into a bowl and then stick the Twix fingers into the ice cream at a dramatic angle. Break up the flake so it's all in tiny pieces and then pour maple syrup over everything. This is frikkin awesome and the perfect finish to a meal or little treat.

TV shows that are good to watch while eating this:
Predator 2, Challengers, Monkey Man, or anything starring Jason Statham.

Quick Q&A
Q: Could I please swop the Twix to a different chocolate bar, as I'm not that keen on Twix...
A: You can use a Toffee Crisp.

Q: How do you make ice cream?
A: I think it's a combination of ice and cream, but I could be wrong.

Simpleton's Strawberry Cheesecake

There's absolutely no messing about with this recipe. All you need is five minutes to make it.

Sounds good to me, but what do you need to make it?

You'll need the following ingredients:
(This is for a single portion. Just increase quantities to feed more people).

- 2 digestive biscuits mashed up in to crumbs
- Half a cup of zero-fat plain Greek yoghurt
- 1 tablespoon of strawberry jam
- A quarter teaspoon of lemon zest

Now do this...
1. Layer the digestive crumbs into a bowl
2. Put the yoghurt on top of the biscuit crumbs
3. Add the jam on top of that, and then the lemon zest
4. Sprinkle on a few more crumbs

And there you have it. A cheesecake without all the hassle. This is actually very healthy for you, which is not a common phrase in this book.

Quick Q&A

Q: What is lemon zest?
A: it's the outer layer of the lemon. Use a grater on the side of a lemon to get your zest for the above recipe.

Q: I don't like this recipe
A: Technically, that is not an actual question. But if you don't like this recipe, you can make a formal complaint if you think it is affecting your human rights. Write to: The EU Human Rights Commission, 3rd floor, Above the Job Centre, Hull.

My great Uncle Ted, a keen boxer, invented the strawberry cheesecake back in 1953. His boxing record was 35 knock outs, 1 draw, and 1 win.

Rocky Road using Twix
or Toffee Crisp

When I first started doing this cookbook, I just wanted to include dead simple instructions and recipes that would help someone who was fucking clueless. But you know what? I thought it might be good to include a few little things that people could progress on to if they were feeling a bit more adventurous than using a microwave.

This great little recipe will take about 20 minutes to make and about five minutes to cook. It takes about an hour and a half to set and is easy to do.

This is perfect if you have some people coming to stay or just want to stuff your face whilst watching your favourite Netflix drama.

I think I actually prefer using toffee crisps for this, but you can do whatever you like, as it'll be you who's eating it.

What do you need?

- Golden syrup 160g
- milk chocolate 425g
- Unsalted butter 125 g
- Mini marshmallows 110g
- Shortbread 165g
- Twix 325g

How to make it...

1. Get a nine-inch square tin and put some greaseproof paper in it.
2. Break up your Twix bars and shortbread into small pieces and then stick it all into a decent-sized bowl. Now add your marshmallows. It's all coming together now, isn't it?
3. Now it's time to put the syrup and butter into a pan on a medium heat until the butter has melted. The syrup can be a pain in the arse to measure out, but you have to do it, or the recipe won't work.
4. Once that's sorted, take your pan off the heat and put the chocolate in and keep stirring it until it's smooth. You can always add it back on the hob for a few minutes if the chocolate hasn't melted properly.
5. When you've done all that, leave the mixture to cool for a couple of minutes and then pour it all into your bowl. Stir it up and then pour into your tin. If you've got any Twix left over, put this on top and then leave the tin in the fridge to set until it's solid. That's it, you've done.

*This recipe is a version of one used by janespattisserie.com but I've changed it a bit as I thought there was too much sugar and stuff like that in it.

This recipe is perfect to eat while you're watching one of those brilliant dramas of More 4, (Walter Presents such as The Bridge, or The Adulterer. Both are brilliant. This recipe is also pretty good even if you've got the telly Chocolate cake for dummies turned off. It's so versatile!

True story...

The last time I made some of this rocky road, I was going to watch a Bruce Willis movie. I found the DVD case but there was no disc inside so I couldn't watch Armageddon. Still, it's not the end of the world…

Ice Cream Surprise!

Here's a great pudding to make which is simplicity itself, yet looks really good, so if you're looking to impress someone, then this could be the one for you. To be honest, this pudding is great at any time.

All you need is:

- Some soft scoop ice cream from your favourite supermarket
- Sugar waffles (Aldi's are great. I know I mention Aldi quite a lot, but that's because there's one at the end of my road, so I tend to go there quite a bit.
- Maple syrup (Tesco do a brilliant one – I think it's in the baking section, but I could be wrong. It's not expensive at all. I've just googled it, and it's called Zero Calorie Maple Syrup by The Skinny Food Co.
- Your favourite chocolate bar. I use a toffee crisp, me.

To make:
Put some ice cream in a bowl. Toast the waffles. Add some syrup. And then get a cheese grater and rub your chocolate on to it and 'shred' it over the top of the waffle and ice cream. It's as simple as that.

*If you want to be a little healthier, then replace the chocolate bar with some blueberries or strawberries. Even fruit tastes good in this dish. It's a winner.

Subjects which are good to talk about whilst eating this dish:

- Movies
- Married at First Sight TV show
- Local transport issues

Did you know?

Ice cream was invented by Reginald Whippy in Huddersfield in 1877... unfortunately it was a disaster, as the fridge-freezer wasn't invented until 1976. I read this online somewhere...

Lemon & Blueberry Muffins

These are absolutely delicious. I originally tried the recipe on janespatisserie.com but changed some of the quantities. I could (and have) easily eaten a dozen of these at one sitting, they are so moreish.

Ingredients for the muffins

- 110g of unsalted butter
- 2 eggs
- 220g caster sugar
- 125ml of whole milk (blue cap)
- Zest of 2 lemons (that's the rough outside bit of the lemon)
- 240 g of self-raising flour
- 200g of blueberries

Decoration them...

- 75g icing sugar
- 1-2 tbsp of lemon juice
- 100g blueberries
- A bit more can they have a lemon zest

What do you do?

1. Preheat your oven to 180C and get a muffin tray ready – this means put those little paper cases in, ready.
2. Now Rocky road using twix mix the unsalted butter and caster sugar together until it's all nice and smooth. This will take about 3 three minutes if you're using a fork r something, or just a few seconds if you're going to use an electric mixer thing.
3. Add in the eggs and milk a bit at a time until it's all mixed in nicely.
4. Now put in the self-raising flour with the salt and mix again until the mixture is all combined. This is dead easy to do.
5. Now, in most cookery books they tell you 'fold in' the ingredients, but I think the word 'mix' is just as good, don't you? So now I'd like you to mix in the lemon zest and blueberries. When you've done that, pour the mixture as evenly as you can into the 12 muffin cases that you got ready a few minutes ago.
6. Bake in the oven for 25 minutes until cooked and then let them cool in the tin for a bit. Of course, if they're not done after 25 minutes, let them bake for another 5 minutes or so, until they are.

Did you know?
The EU once tried to ban the word muffin because it sounded a bit rude. I remember when Channel 4 tried to ban The Vagina Monologues on TV. They took it off the air and replaced it with the Guy Richie movie 'Snatch'.

What about decorating them?

Once your lovely muffins have cooled down, whisk the icing sugar and lemon juice together until it's quite thick.

Dollop some on top of each individual muffin and plonk a few blueberries into the icing sugar mix. For an added flourish, sprinkle a bit of lemon zest over the top, and this will stick into the icing sugar and make it look all professional!

Advice

Only use fresh blueberries for this because they make it taste much better than frozen ones. Honestly, what are you pulling a face like that for? Just trust me.

What about doing this?

I think muffins are great with custard on. Why not try it I bet you'll love it. Use any shop-bought custard for this tasty treat.

Celebrities who I think would absolutely love a lemon and blueberry muffin include: Mick Jagger, lead singer of the Rolling Stones. Artist David Hockney and politician Penny Mordaunt.

Biscuit Management

Every flat or house needs a ready supply of biscuits and a bit further down I will be recommending some of the best biscuits on the market. But first, let's tackle the controversial subject of biscuit storage.

Some people have a plastic jar with a screw lid on it, like they do in Richard Curtis movies. (I swear I saw one in the movie Notting Hill). Anyway, these are OK if you live at home, but if you're a student, do you really want to lug a biscuit jar all the way to Loughborough University? No, I thought not.

Anyway, I sometimes think that if you put loose biscuits in a jar, they all tend to start smelling the same, no matter which flavour they're supposed to be.

A good tip is to eat all the biscuits straight away as soon as you get back from the shops, then you won't have to worry about storing them anywhere.

Let's be serious for a minute

Focus on buying biscuits that are individually wrapped because these keep fresher for longer. Biscuits like KitKats, Twix, all those Aldi biscuits which are like Mars bars but are called something else… there are lots to choose from, and you can put them all into a tin or something like that without the fear of cross contamination.

Here are my top 5 favourite biscuits.

- Tunnock's Marshmallows.
- Kitkat (orange flavour)
- Tunnock's Caramel Wafers
- Caramel Digestives
- Custard Creams

*I almost included Wagon Wheels, which are an absolute classic. In fact, I wish I'd included them instead of Custard Creams now, but it's too late, I think.

Top biscuit tip

If you have a packet of biscuits already opened, twist the packaging and put it up against the wall to stop it unwrapping itself.

When is the best time to have a biscuit?

I personally think the best time is about ten minutes after you've had your evening meal with a cup of tea or coffee. But that's just me. You can have one whenever you like, with my full blessing. I think the worst time to have a biscuit is probably when you're scuba diving that would be a fucking nightmare. Just wait 'til you get back on the boat.

Quick Q&A

Questions sent in via social media by real people...

Q: What is the last time of the day that you can have a biscuit?

A: Good question. We asked Professor Digestive of the European Biscuit Commission in Brussels, but he was actually on annual leave, so we're non-the-wiser.

Q: Is it acceptable to eat a biscuit half an hour before your tea?

A: Yes, because your tea is usually late anyway, so you'll be alright, I think.

Q&A *Questions sent in online from real people with nothing better to do...*

Q: Why the fuck are blueberries so expensive?
A: Because blueberries grow right at the top of the blueberry tree, which means the pickers need to have extra-long ladders – and all this adds to the cost... plus, there are big legal bills to pay for when blueberry pickers fall off the ladder etc.

Q: Are blueberry stains difficult to get out of white undergarments?
A: According to my next door neighbour, Jean, YES! She recommends making a hole in a black bin liner and putting your head through it when eating blueberries, so you are safe from potential stains. She always uses this 'device' when she's out in a posh restaurant.

Bonkers for Blueberries
This is a traybake thing

I love blueberries, me. In fact, my all-time favourite pie is blueberry. It's really popular in America, but you don't find it much in the UK, which is a shame. Here's a blueberry thing you can make. It's especially good if you're trying to impress someone. Or even if you're not.

This is what you need:
- 200g of unsalted butter
- 4 eggs
- 200g caster sugar
- 200g plain flour
- 250 white chocolate chips
- 250g of blueberries
- 125g of white chocolate (melted)

Instructions
1. Turn on your oven (that's the big thing in the kitchen that has a frying pan on top of it!). Turn it to 180C (160C if you have a fan oven).
   While it's heating up, line a tin which measures 9 x 9 inches with greaseproof paper and rub some butter on it this is where your mixture will go in a minute!
2. First thing you need to do is melt your butter in the microwave until it's soft and then give it a stir, then leave it for a minute…
3. Melt the butter in the microwave, or in a pan, and stir until smooth. Leave to cool slightly on the side.
4. Hang on.
5. Now, do you know a 'whisk' is? (Google it!). Whisk (or use a fork, right fast) the eggs together with the caster sugar for about 4 minutes until it's much thicker. Once it has about doubled in volume, you'll know it's about right!
   There's a little trick you can use to see if it's ready: Lift the whisk up and the mixture will take a few seconds to sink back in to the rest of the mixture it's really not difficult.
6. Slowly pour in the butter as you continue to mix it. DO THIS SLOWLY and GRADUALLY. If you don't, I will come round house and slash your tyres.
   OK, once you've done that nice and SLOWLY, add the flour and mix it all in. Then add the chocolate chips and around half of the blueberries. You're almost done!
7. Bake in the oven for 35-45 minutes, or until its baked through. Sometimes it can take a bit longer as some ovens vary a bit. Plus, it can take a bit longer if you haven't whisked it enough when you were preparing it.
8. When they're done, let them cool in the baking tin for a bit. Then take them out of the tin carefully and pour the melted chocolate over them. You might want to add some sprinkles as well, or you might not.
   Once you've left it for a couple of hours and it's all set, you can cut it up into squares and then consume like a ravenous wolf.
9. Sometimes traybakes can take a while to bake, for some random reason, and even NASA don't know why! So, if at 35-45 minutes yours isn't baked through fully, cover it with foil and bake it for longer until it's done.

*These will last for a week in one of those Chinese takeaway container things.

PUDDINGS & STUFF

I wasn't going to put any puddings in this book because I'd actually got fed up of writing it, but them the publishers said, "Hold your fucking horses, you've got another twenty pages to fill!" So, I've put some puddings and stuff together so that you're not faced with loads of blank pages.

Crumpet Cheese & Bacon Toastie

This is another quick sandwich idea that is tasty and quick to make. As long as you have a toasted sandwich maker, you'll be fine. If you don't have one, then you're up shit creek. And no, you don't have a paddle, either.

What do you need?
2 crumpets
Some butter
Bacon
2 x Cheese slices

How do you make it?
Take two crumpets and place them side-by-side
On top of one of them, spread some butter on it, then place 2 rashers of cooked bacon (do these just how you like them), then place 2 cheese slices on top of the bacon. Then place the other crumpet of top of the cheese. Now place the lot into the sandwich maker and close the lid.
*You can replace the bacon with already cooked ham slices if you prefer. This is quicker than cooking bacon.

Quick Q&A

*Real questions sent in online by real people...

Q: **What actually is a crumpet?**
A: I think it's some sort of a... no, hang on... actually, I'm not sure.

Q: **I don't like crumpets, so can I make something else instead?**
A: No, not if you're making this recipe.

Cinnamon Butter Toast

Here's a great yet dead simple recipe for when you come at 4am and the effect of your kebab has almost worn off. Make some cinnamon butter and stick it on your toast. It's even easier if you made it earlier and it's already in the fridge for you this is a big favourite in America.

You'll need...
- A cup of butter. The size of cup is up to you. Make sure the butter is quite soft or it'll be a nightmare.
- 2 ounces of granulated sugar
- 2 ounces of brown sugar
- 4 teaspoons of ground cinnamon

1. Once you've got your ingredients ready, mix them all together until it's all nice and smooth. That's it.
2. Cover with Clingfilm and (that's the cinnamon butter, not you) and stand in the fridge overnight. (Again, that's the cinnamon butter, not you).
3. When you're ready for some, simply make some toast and spread some of your cinnamon butter on it. This is a fantastic treat, and you can pretend you're in America while eating it.

Quick Q&A
Q: What is cinnamon butter on toast good with?
A: A lovely cup of tea. But, if you've just come in after an eight-hour drinking binge, it'll taste good with virtually anything cos you'll be too pissed to remember.

Q: Is cinnamon toast healthy?
A: Yes, it is, according to cinnamon sugar manufacturers

Q: What sort of bread is the best to put it on?
A: For many recipes in this 'award-winning' book, I have bigged-up cheap white bread, but for cinnamon butter, I am going to shock you. This is best with nice brown bread. And I haven't even been drinking.

Corned Beef Sandwich

Corned beef is always useful to have in your cupboard because it comes in a tin and virtually lasts forever. So, when you roll in after an eight-hour sesh, and your fridge is empty you can knock up a corned beef sandwich in 2 minutes.

Warning: As corned beef comes in a tin with sharp edges, the chances of you ending up in A&E are extremely high, but you're most likely to be drunk anyway, so the potential danger will not put you off.

What will you need?
- A tin of corned beef
- Some bread and butter or spread.
- Open the tin using the little key which is usually fixed to the side of the tin. Once you've opened it, you'll probably need to use a knife around the inner edges to ease out the corned beef itself. Ideally, corned beef is best once it's been in the fridge for a bit because it's easier to slice. But it's not the end of the world if you use it straight out of the cupboard.
- Corned beef is great with a friend egg!
- If you cannot open your tin of corned beef, then keep it hand at the side of your bed as it may come in useful to throw at burglars etc.

Quick Question:

Q: What IS corned beef?
A: We approached CAMRA (the Campaign for Real Ale) and they told us we'd rung the wrong department, so as things stand at the moment, we have no idea what corned beef actually is.

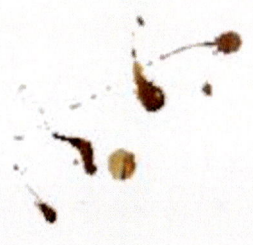

The author in his special outfit knitted out of corned beef left-overs.

Pasty Butty

Many years ago, I used to work with a guy called Matt who was very artistic when it came to making sandwiches. He loved putting a pie or a pasty between two slices of bread and revelled in his own creativeness. And when he was eating his pie sarnie, he was in ecstasy. No one could ever have enjoyed it more. Of course, the other guys in the office used to laugh at his lunchtime antics, but perhaps we were secretly jealous of his creations.

Matt was ahead of his time, I think. Now, his ideas would probably make him a Michelin-star chef or at the very least he'd be a viral sensation.

When I was thinking about guilty pleasures for this book, Matt sprung to mind, so I thought it was worth mentioning. After all, if an idea is still memorable all these years later, then it must be a good idea, eh?

Try these out:
A Greggs pasty sandwich
A Greggs sausage roll and chip butty combo
A pie sandwiches. Steak and kidney is a must
A cheese and onion pasty sandwich

Heath note: *A sandwich like this is probably not very healthy for you, but I will wager that after a night out drinking heavily, you will not give a flying fuck about calories.*

*When eating a pasty sandwich, the best music to listen to is Pink Floyd the Dark side of the moon album.

Chip Butty

A chip butty is hard to beat. This takes me back to my school days when we all went out at lunchtime and spent our parent's hard-earned money in a cholesterol-induced combination of potatoes and lard.

A chip butty is a working-class classic which totally satisfies. And these days they are so easy to make, thanks to oven chips.

I know I keep going on about white bread and how it must be used for certain types of sandwiches, and this is another one where you should never use brown bread or one of those fancy loaves. It has to be sliced, white bread for the ultimate in authenticity.

You need:
- Sliced white bread and butter
- Your favourite oven chips
- Salt
- Sauce

Simply cook your oven chips add salt and then place them into your buttered bread and press down to squash them a bit so they don't fall out. There's no secret to it, it's a doddle.

If you want to bring the chip butty up to date, why not use Piri-Piri salt. You could also melt some cheese in the microwave and then place it over your chips once they're in the bread. Awesome. Stick a fried egg in there too if you're sober enough to do it.

Fried Egg Sarnie

This is one of the all-time great sarnies. It's the main reason why we won two world wars single-handedly.

You may think, 'hang on a minute Graham, any twat can fry an egg!' but unfortunately, you'll be wrong. But… the good news is that it's not difficult. Remember – this book is for people who probably can't even spell the word kitchen, let alone enter it and make something edible. Just go with the flow.

All you need for this classic is some eggs, some white bread, butter and the sauce of your choice. I prefer tomato sauce for this. Heinz is the best ketchup by far, but I know it costs more than a fucking Tesla to buy a bottle these days, so I will forgive you if you go for a cheaper version.

1. Butter your bread. Use real butter if you can.
2. Put some vegetable oil in the frying pan. And turn on the hob.
3. Put your eggs into the pan now before the oil gets hot – that way you'll get perfect fried eggs every time. Now, as they are frying nicely in the pan, get a spoon and keep putting some of the oil on top of the eggs. This makes them cook evenly and gives the yolk a white topping, which is how farmers have their eggs. Once all the 'white' of the eggs has solidified which probably takes three or four minutes, your eggs will be done.

If you like your yolks runny, then take them out earlier, if you like your yolks a little harder, then fry them a bit longer. You can see by looking at the yolks how well done they are. Just do them how you like them, and then put them onto your prepared bread. Add your sauce, cut in half and you're done.

*Add a bit of salt and pepper for the perfect finish

*This is my brother's favourite thing to eat. He has a lot of issues… he has this overwhelming desire to swear every time he's near a castle. Apparently, he's got turrets syndrome…

Eggy Bread

This is a bit of an underrated classic. It's quick, versatile and is good with ketchup on if you're that way inclined.

1. Coat a frying pan with melted butter and have the pan on a medium heat.
2. Put a few eggs in a bowl and stir them up so the yolks are broken.
3. Get a slice of white bread and dip it into the egg mixture. Then place the bread into the frying pan and fry until it's how you want it on one side. Then turn it over and cook the other side. *That's the bread, not the whole frying pan!*

Tip
If you've got some bacon already cooked, then do two slices of eggy bread and place some bacon between them.

Baked Camembert

This is a very easy thing to make. I think my brother showed me this years ago, and since then, I've seen quite a few TV chefs doing similar stuff. This is a versatile dish you could just have this as a main meal if you want, or it's perfect as a starter or if you're having a buffet…

What do you need?
- A camembert cheese (or brie)
- Flaked almonds
- Apricot jam
- Fresh, crusty bread

1. First, cut off the 'top' of the camembert cheese and bin it. Put the cheese back in it's wooden or bamboo casing. Now spread apricot jam on top of the cheese. Make this nice and thick. Then sprinkle almond flakes over the top of the jam.
2. All you have to do now is put the camembert in some foil, fastened loosely on top. Now stick it on a baking tray and place on a pre-heated oven on a medium heat (about 180 degrees) for about 20/25 minutes. It should be nice and bubbly by then. If it's not, then give it a few more minutes.
3. Dip in your crusty bread to ram it into your gob. Perfect.

Dip in your crusty bread and ram it into your gob. Perfect.

*Instead of apricot jam and almonds, you could sprinkle on some chilli flakes! But be careful not to put too many on.

How to do a Baked Potato

I always think of baked potatoes as either for bonfire night or for people in the 1980's getting something for their lunch whilst they popped out from work. And it was always a baked potato with either coleslaw or chilli on.

The good thing about baked potatoes is that they are really easy to do. You can do them entirely in the microwave if you're not bothered about having the skin all burnt and crispy.

What you need:
A potato, butter, olive oil, salt and pepper.

Preparation time: Not long.

Let's do this!
1. Take your potato and use either a fork or a knife to puncture it a few times. Then stick it in the microwave. The time it takes depends on how big your spud is and how powerful your microwave is. So give it 3 mins or so, then turn it over and give it in another 3 minutes. Then test it by sticking a knife in it. If the knife goes through easily, then take it out of the microwave.
2. The next bit is what gives it a lovely crispy skin really quickly. My friend Nigel at number 44 showed me this and I've done it ever since. Stick on your oven to 200 degrees and place your potato on a baking tray and drizzle olive oil over it. Then add salt and pepper on top.
3. Now stick it in there for 20 or so minutes and you'll see you get a lovely crispy skin. If it needs a bit longer, then leave it in and just keep checking on it.
4. Then when it done, cut open your spud and add a chunk of butter. That, my friends, is a top-quality baked tatie.

TOP tips
You don't have to use baking potatoes – any sort of white potato will do the trick. If you are not bothered about high appliance bills – if you're a student, for example, and you have all your bills included, then I suggest you cook your baked potatoes in the oven and don't bother with the microwave (unless you're in a rush to go out).

In fact, I suggest you heat your whole house using the oven. Let's face it, those landlords can afford it.

Sainsbury's have a great baked potato seasoning you can put on. Other supermarkets sell similar ones.

Good fillings for a baked potato include:
Beans with cheese on top
Chilli with cheese on top
Coleslaw
Coronation chicken (oh, google it)
Bacon and cheese

Celebrities we think would enjoy a nice baked potato:
Singer Charlotte Church, funny man Jim Carey, and outrageous singer Lady GaGa.

Ultra-Quick Garlic Bread

Garlic bread is the perfect accompaniment with lots of different types of meals, but it is also great on its own while you have a glass of wine or beer.
Here's a fantastic and really easy way to make garlic bread. I saw this online and it works like a dream.

What will you need?
Some flour tortillas
Some cheese
Some butter
Some garlic granules

Go on then, tell us how to make it...
1. First, turn on your oven so that it's nice and hot.
2. Get a tortilla wrap (whatever size you like) and spread a bit of butter on it. Then add lots of grated cheese. On top of the cheese, sprinkle some garlic granules. Don't over-do it as garlic is quite strong.
3. Next, add another wrap on top of the one you've just prepared, spread butter and then add more cheese and garlic granules.
4. Finally, add another wrap, spread butter and add cheese and garlic granules. Now stick it in the oven for 5-10 minutes until it's just how you like it. This will come out like a garlic pizza. Really tasty and dead easy to make.

One-minute alternative:

Toast some sourdough bread. Spread some real butter on it and sprinkle on some garlic granules. That's all you have to do.

Interesting fact
Garlic was given to wounded soldiers in WWII as it was known as 'Russian Penicillin'. That is actually true – I read it online. This is always worth mentioning when you're at the doctor's and there's a lull in conversation.

Cauliflower Cheese

There are two, no wait, three ways of making cauliflower cheese. I'm going to tell you a bit about each one.

Firstly, you can buy a bag of cauliflower cheese in Aldi for about a quid. It's not bad, but it does take about 45 minutes to cook it in the oven, which is way too long.

The second way is to cook a cauliflower as normal and then when it's done and you've drained all the water off, stick some Dairylea cheese spread in the pan and move it about until it's melted. Honestly, that really works well.

The last way of making cauliflower cheese is to cook your cauliflower as normal and then get a packet of cheese mix. You just pour it in a pan with some milk and keep stirring it until it looks like an amazing cheese sauce. Check the packet for full details etc, but honestly, it's an absolute doddle.

Some people might tell you that *"in Australia"* they do roast cauliflower and it's the best way of doing cauliflower. I say fuck the Australians. They're obsessed with Kale whatever *that* is, so don't listen to such shit.

Cauliflower quickies...

*Questions submitted online by real people...

Q: **What is cauliflower made of?**
A: No one knows.

Q: **Will cauliflower make you live longer?**
A: "Cauliflower is potentially good for you" according to my mate Terry who works in Next.

Q: **How long does a cauliflower take to cook?**
A: Good question! It varies, depending on how high you have the hob or gas turned up to. When it's a bit soft, it's about done.

Q: **Where do cauliflowers grow?**
A: Probably on a cauliflower tree or something like that.

How do you cook chicken?

I know that some of you worry about killing yourself and others by not cooking your chicken properly. So, I thought it might be good idea to tell you how I do it. It may save lives!

In the oven
The best way is put your chicken breast in some foil. Scrunch the foil loosely around the chicken and then put it on a tray in the over 190 degrees for about 25 minutes. Then take it out and cut in to it. It should be nice and tender AND COOKED! It should be juicy and tasty.

Fry it
Place your chicken in a frying pan with some vegetable oil and turn it over a time or two and cook it on a medium/high heat for five minutes. I then cut the breast up into smaller bite-size pieces and fry those for ten or fifteen minutes. I use scissors to cut them up as once they're partly cooked, they are much easier to cut up.

When you cut into your 'cooked' chicken it should be white NOT pink or pinkish. You'll know the difference. If there is any pink to it, cook it for longer. It's not difficult but it is important. Call me old fashioned but I'd like my readers to have long and fruitful, well-cooked-chicken lives.

Quick Q&A

Q: Please could you show me a photo of some well-cooked chicken?
A: Yes, see photo…

If you don't cook your chicken properly, you could find yourself being air-lifted to hospital in a helicopter. Once at the hospital, be prepared for a three-week wait in a corridor. Amusingly, while you're waiting, they have lovely chicken sandwiches on sale in the hospital shop!

Gravy – what's that all about?

When the food on your plate is a bit dry, then you could be lacking what we professionals call "gravy." Gravy is made out of little granules. No one knows what's in those granules – even the makers, as they never replied to my email – so let's just crack on without their input.

What is gravy good on?
Gravy is good on top of something like chicken. It can also be good on Yorkshire puddings. It's also very good if you have a pie that needs enhancing. If you are going to go into town and get pissed, you'll find that at about 3am, you'll get a weird desire to have a polystyrene tray of chips and baked beans with loads of gravy on from Stavros's mobile kebab van.

How do you make gravy?
Pour some granules into a jug and then pour some boiling water in and mix it until it's as thick as you like it. Then it's ready to pour on stuff.

Celebrities who like gravy possibly include:
Will I Am, Lord of the Rings director Peter Jackson and actor Joanna Lumley

Celebrities we think probably don't like gravy include:
Rita Ora and ex-athlete Steve Cram.

Other uses for gravy gone wrong:
Gouting or fake sun-tan.

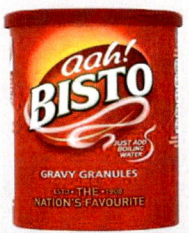

Quick Q&A

Questions submitted online by real people.

Q: Is it legal to mop up your gravy using bread?
A: Yes, it's perfectly legal according to a top barrister.

Q: I am holding a very posh party and wondered whether to bother doing gravy or not - as it will help avoid anyone getting splashes on their expensive outfits. What do you think?
A: Great idea, although I think that if you make your gravy thick enough, you can just give each guest a 'blob' of gravy, thus avoiding embarrassing splashes and the like.

Q: Is there a good gravy substitute I could use instead of gravy?
A: I don't understand the question.

Having Guests Round?

Firstly, I would do your best to discourage guests from coming round to your house, as it only means more work for you. From cleaning the toilet to making sure you've got enough crisps in, it's one thing after another. And it's going to cost you.

Here are a few good excuses that you can give in order to prevent having people round your house:

1. "I'm afraid I've got a massive dose of diarrhoea and it's like a tsunami at the moment. There's not a room in the house that isn't splattered with my DNA…"
2. "It will be great to see you… I'll be in the middle of painting the whole house and I'll make sure there are spare brushes so you can get stuck in for a few hours…"
3. "I've been informed by my friend Barry, who works in The Pentagon, that there's a nuclear war starting in the next few hours, so I'm going to be busy digging a nuclear shelter…"
4. "I'm afraid I'm busy at the moment… the police are here asking about a few of my friends that have disappeared recently…"
5. "My grandma and grandad are also visiting so you can meet them. They're naturists, by the way…"
6. "Excellent. You can help me with my 'anal-bleaching' session while you're here…"

If you simply cannot stop your friends coming round, then here's a list of things you need to do before they arrive:

- Put away all your sex toys
- Make sure your toilet is skid-mark free
- Hide all your best booze
- Hide any drugs
- Leave out a box pf paracetamol so you can claim to have a migraine and then kick them out…

If the FBI knock on your door and they are armed, then I would recommend you let them in and give them a big helping of your signature dish. That should stop them shooting you.

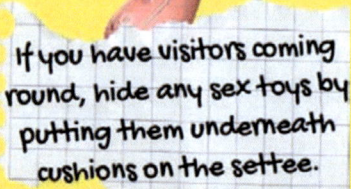

If you have visitors coming round, hide any sex toys by putting them underneath cushions on the settee.

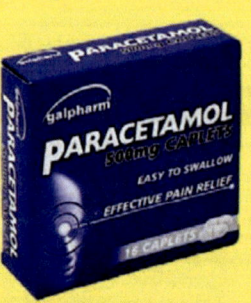

The Perfect Chilli

Here's my recipe for a chilli. It's simple doesn't take long at all. You can freeze the leftovers or just bung it in the fridge until tomorrow. And remember, for some reason, chilli always seems to taste better the next day.

Ingredients:
- An onion, a pepper, some beef mince (or Quorn), some tomato ketchup, garlic, and a jar of passata and a packet of Old El Passo chilli mix. Oh, nearly forgot the fucking kidney beans. OK, that's the magical formula.
- And you'll need some rice.
- Possible extras to give it a lift: Sour cream, grated cheese, tortilla chips and salsa.

I make my chilli in a wok, because it makes me feel like I know what I'm doing. I'm sure that in Mexico, when the workers come in after a hard day's work for the drug's cartel, they'll wolf down a bowl of chilli just like this. My chilli is so authentic, you can almost taste the cocaine – although I must tress that I do not use cocaine or any other drugs in my chilli recipe.

Let's get cracking...
1. Cut up your onion and your pepper and fry it in a pan with some vegetable oil and a chopped-up garlic clove. Once the onion has gone 'transparent', add the minced beef. Once it's cooked, add the passata, the drained kidney beans, a couple of squirts of tomato ketchup and a packet of Old El Passo chilli mix. Now give it a few stirs, and let it bubble away for 20 or 30 mins.
2. **For the basmati rice:** Put your rice into a pan of boiling water and simmer for about 12 minutes. When it's soft, it's ready. Rinse with boiling water, and you're all set. Fluffy rice here we come. Or, if you're too lazy to bother with cooking your own rice, microwave some Uncle Ben's or similar.

Did you know?
Chilli is a popular dish all over the world, but I'm told that in South America they absolutely fucking love it.

Make your chilli whilst listening to:
I think a bit of Meatloaf (Bat out of Hell album) is perfect. But power ballads by REO Speedwaggon or even something by 70's glam-rockers Slade will also do the trick. If I were you, I'd steer clear of anything by Harry Styles as it's not quite the right vibe. And don't play anything by Sam Smith, cos he's shits.

Serve with: A tin of re-fried beans.

Tip: Take the re-fried beans out of the tin before heating and serving.

I like to add some sour cream and grated cheese once it's served, and believe me, this tastes fantastic.

*Don't be tempted to use any other type of chilli mix except Old El Paso. All the best supermarkets sell it, and it's brilliant.

Quick Q&A *Questions submitted online by people with issues

Q: What are oven chips made of?
A: Potatoes, generally

Q: How long are oven chips in length?
A: They tend to vary, depending on length

Q: Can you use ketchup with oven chips
A: Yes, but only if you like ketchup.

Q: Where do you store your oven chips?
A: In the freezer, in the second compartment down. Usually underneath a bag of peas.

Q: If I make too many oven chips, do I have to eat them all?
A: That depends on how hungry you are, but as a rule, the answer is 'yes' – unless you don't want to, then the answer is 'no'.

Q: For a dinner party how many oven chips should each guest be served, as a general rule?
A: No more than 20 each say the experts.

The Oven Chips Conundrum Explained

We've all fucked-up with oven chips at one time or another, haven't we? And many people still struggle with them, so now I am going to give you the secrets to cooking brilliant oven chips. That's right, hold on to your hats my explosive expose of oven chips is about to change your life.

When oven chips were first announced to the world by Mr McCain, or whoever it was, it seemed like all our catering woes were over. But not so. Oven chips have seemed to create more problems than ever. Many people seem to struggle with the simplest of instructions and have no concept of common sense especially people in Huddersfield, but that's an issue for social services rather than this cookbook.

What's so difficult about doing oven chips? Well, there are issues such as: Do you need to turn them over during cooking? Can they overlap each other? Can you mix the French fries' variety with the chunky, thick cut type? It's an absolute minefield.

The most important thing to do is ignore the cooking time they give on the packet they are never done properly after sticking to the guidelines. I would like to attack whoever wrote them with a rusty claw-hammer. OK, you may say that is a slight over-reaction, but I don't think so. Whatever time they give you on the packet – add another 10 minutes.

To be brutally honest, I never even look at the packet anymore, I just put them in the oven until they are going brown and crispy. Then I try one, and if it tastes nice, then they're done.

Tip
Oven chips taste nice with: Pie, beans, peas, fish fingers, in a butty, in fact they are one of the most versatile foods on the planet, according to online forums. Oven chips taste great with mayonnaise. I recently bought a jar of mayo and it said, "stand in a cool place" – so I went to Cuba!

Here are my guidelines to cooking oven chips. Ignore these at your peril:

1. Put the oven chips on a tray which has sides. Otherwise, when you try and turn them over, some of them will fall out and get wedged in the hinge bit where the door closes. And they will stay there forever.
2. Turn the chips over once. You don't want them all bronzed on one side yet looking whiter than a Klu Klux Klan meeting on the other. Get those chips looking bronzed.
3. That's it.

Useful info:
Don't microwave oven chips, as they taste shit.

Celebrities who may like oven chips include:
Teresa May, Chris Martin (from Coldplay), Dr John Sentamu (ex-Archbishop of York).

Celebrities who possibly don't like them:
Newsreader Naga Munchetty, footballer Mo Salah, and brainy celebrity Stephen Fry.

Calorie count:
See pack for details.

Vegetables: Are they really necessary?

This is a tough question, as no one really likes vegetables, but they feel like they have to say they do, or they'll look like a twat.

I believe that vegetables are actually OK in certain circumstances. With a roast dinner for example, some carrots and peas are worth having on your plate and eating first before you get stuck into the good stuff (Yorkshire puds/meat).

My tip for veg is to buy frozen stuff wherever you can (apart from broccoli, which is always crap from frozen). Frozen veg is much cheaper than fresh stuff that you normally end up throwing away.

How do you cook veg?

Put it in boiling water until it's ready. And by ready, I mean until it's a bit soft, but definitely not mushy. If you're feeling flush, then you can buy some veg which is in a bag, and you just microwave it.

Vegetarians

There are some people who actually don't eat meat – and I'm being totally serious here! So, all they eat is vegetables and things which don't have meat in, such as rhubarb. What sort of life is that, I sometimes ask myself – but then I get distracted and don't think about it again.

If you like vegetables, a good tip is to put a knob of butter on them before serving, and add some salt and black pepper. That helps them taste better, I think.

These orange things are called carrots, I believe.

Here is a list of vegetables you might like to try:

- Peas
- Cauliflower
- Carrots
- Potatoes
- There are others as well, but they escape me for the moment.

Annoying Celebrities who may, or may not be vegetarians:

Celebrity, Stacey Solomon
Emma Atkins, Emmerdale's Charity Dingle
Liverpool footballer Mo Salah
R.E.M lead singer Michael Stipe

How to make the world's best Yorkshire puddings

For years, I struggled to make the perfect Yorkshire puds. My mum always made one big one rather than 12 small ones and it always seemed to work for her, but I have no idea what her secret was, because when I was a kid, I didn't give a fuck about Yorkshire puddings, but I do now. Anyway, a few years ago, a brilliant chef invited me into a back room and offered to show me his 'secret' – and I'm pleased to say he served 8 months for his behaviour. When he was released, he offered to show me how to make the perfect mixture. It's incredibly easy. And if I say so, then it really must be.

How to make the perfect mixture: I'm presuming you have one of those baking trays that hold 12 smaller Yorkshire puddings.

1. Firstly, get yourself a standard drinking cup. You'll be using this for measuring the amounts you don't need scales or anything fancy like that.
2. Now fill the cup to the top with plain flour. If you don't have any, you CAN use self-rising flour. I once ran out of plain flour so used self-rising flour and the puddings still rose impressively. Anyhow, now pour this, and THEN ANOTHER HALF A CUP into a mixing bowl or whatever you have handy. So, that's one and a half cups of plain flour.
3. Now do EXACTLY the same with milk (I use semi-skimmed, but any will do). And pour that into your mixing bowl. Now do the same again with eggs – although just a single cup full of eggs will be fine rather than a cup and a half.
4. Now add some salt and pepper. And then mix all the contents together by hand for a minute. That's the mixture all done. See, I told you it was easy! It will probably be a bit lumpy, but don't panic, that's OK.

Top tip
You can freeze the spare puddings. Then, when you need them, just stick them into the oven for 5 mins and you have perfect puddings for any occasion - from a Sunday dinner to a surprise royal visitor!

Getting your oven and stuff ready:
1. Turn the oven on to 190/195 degrees if it's a fan oven.
2. Pour some vegetable oil into each of the 12 compartments in your tray – don't go overboard – just enough so all the bottom is covered in each one. Then shove it in the oven for five mins until the oil is hot. Then take the tray out and pour the pudding mixture into each compartment 'til it's almost level to the top. Now place it back in the oven for about 40 minutes. Don't open the oven door, or you're fucked! Those potential prize-winning puddings will deflate faster than a lottery winner who's lost their ticket.
3. That's it. You'll never use another method after you've tried this. When I first tried it, the Yorkshire puddings rose so high that they touched the roof of the oven and burned a bit. So, make sure there's plenty of room for them to rise, cos they will!

Yorkshire puddings are good with:
Vegetables, and something such as a pork joint. Always add gravy, for that certain something…

Things to do while waiting for your Yorkshire puddings to rise:
Listen to some music I've always found that Abba is a sure-fire winner. For those with a different music palette try the Kinks!

Pesto Pasta with bacon and mushrooms

This is a quick and delicious recipe you can make in about 15 minutes. It's idea for when you're rushing in after work or from a busy day shoplifting.

What do you need?
- A packet of your favourite bacon
- Some mushrooms
- Some fresh pasta (or dried stuff)
- Some pesto (about half a jar)
- Salt and pepper
- Garlic granules

*I usually buy the fresh pesto and pasta if possible, which you'll find in the refrigerated section at your favourite supermarket. I don't think Aldo sell fresh pesto, but I could be wrong. I get mine from Tesco, or I make it myself if I can be arsed.

1. Fry the bacon how you like it, and when it's ready, let it cool for a few minutes and then cut it up into little pieces.
2. Fry some mushrooms and then put them to one side, ready.
3. Cook the pasta. If it's fresh it will only take 3 or 4 minutes.
4. Drain the pasta and then add the pesto, bacon, mushrooms and some garlic granules. For a final flourish, sprinkle over some grated pecorino cheese (this comes already grated in little bags. It's a doddle.

This recipe is dedicated to my friend Nigel who's got three children, all named after where they were conceived. He's got Chelsea, who was conceived in Chelsea, Georgia, who was conceived in Georgia, and his youngest is called McDonald's Car Park.

Smoked Mackerel & Rice

This is one of my favourite things, yet until September 2023 I had never even had it. My friend Vicky said she was going to make it, so I basically nicked the idea and now here it is, in my cookbook. Of course, I will be giving her a (very) small percentage of any royalties I receive through sales. However, there's more chance of the Beatles reforming than that happening. But honestly, Vicky says it's OK for me to use her fabulous recipe. She's ace.

I love this recipe because it's dead easy and totally delicious.

What do you need?
- A small thing of single cream.
- Some of your favourite pasta.
- A packet of smoked mackerel from your local supermarket.
- Some salt and some black pepper.
- Some chilli flakes (you can get these from any supermarket, they come in a little bottle).

Prepare
1. Get the mackerel out of the packet and peel the skins off and then break it up into small pieces. Watch out for any stray bones when you do it. To be honest, the thought of finding a fish bone almost put me off making this fucking thing, but it turned out alright in the end, so I'm glad I did it.
2. Cook some rice in boiling water for approximately ten minutes or until it's nice and soft.
3. Then drain the rice, add some cream (as much as you want to) and then put in all the mackerel. Mix it all up, add some salt and black pepper and you're ready to go. This is better than any of those pretentious TV chefs can do. Tasty yet not pretentious.
4. Oh, I nearly forgot! Add a few chilli flakes to give it a little bit of extra taste. The first time I made this I thought I'd got some chilli flakes in the cupboard, but I hadn't. This dish is miles better with chilli flakes, but don't put too many in or you'll blow your head off. Gently does it, my loves.

Quick Q&A

Questions sent in via the internet, by real people, god help us.

Q: What do I do if I see a fish bone?
A: Remove it and put it in the bin
Q: Where does mackerel come from?
A: Tesco, somewhere near the salmon
Q: Can I add anything else in to make this dish a bit better?
A: You could add some peas, that would be nice

Important information: This dish is also great with pasta instead of rice, so the choice is yours. If you're going all out to impress, you could use salmon instead of smoked mackerel. Hmm, I definitely like the sound of that.

Begin layering your lasagne

1. Spread a thin layer of the beef/tomato sauce in the bottom of the baking dish. Cover with about 5 lasagne sheets in the baking dish, breaking them up so it makes a single layer (it's OK if the pasta sheets overlap a bit). Now spread 1 cup of the white sauce over the pasta sheets. Then add about 1 1/2 cups of the meat sauce on the sauce. Basically, you will alternate the layers: Beef/tomato sauce, then lasagne sheets, then white sauce until you've made three complete layers. You are paying attention aren't you, and not messing about on your mobile?
2. Finally, sprinkle a good layer of cheese on top.
   *If you prefer, you can use parmesan or gran Padano on top.
3. Then cover the dish tightly with aluminium foil.
4. Bake the lasagne for 1 hour. But remove the foil after 30 minutes. Check to make sure the pasta sheets are done by poking the lasagne with a knife; the knife should slide easily through all the layers. If it doesn't, cover and cook for 15 minutes more.
5. No one wants a crunchy lasagne. I once undercooked this and I still have sleepless nights about it now.
6. Make sure it's all golden on top and bubbling away. Then all that remains is for you to wolf it down. And why not have some garlic bread with it?

Tip
Make a lasagne sandwich. It's ideal in between 2 slices of white bread and is perfect for that bedtime treat.

NOTES

Make it before you want it: The lasagne can be made and refrigerated up to 2 days in advance, or frozen for up to 1 month. Thaw the frozen lasagne for 2 days in the refrigerator before baking. You can make it into a vegetarian lasagne by replacing the beef with vegetables.

Leftovers can be stored in the refrigerator for up to 3 days.

What do you have with lasagne?

Some people like to have salad with it, but I'd steer clear of anything green. Let's be honest anything that's been grown in the ground could have had a dog pissing on it, or even worse. The best thing you can do is have a huge pile of chips with your lasagne.

Easy Lasagne

The easiest way of getting yourself a nice lasagne is by getting one from Tesco or wherever and all you have to do is puncture the cellophane lid a few times and stick it in the oven. But, if you fancy trying your hand at making one yourself, it's going to take an hour or so to do it.

I don't make lasagne very often because I just can't be arsed, but now and again I'll bite the bullet. I found the recipe below on an American website and I've made it several times and it's sooo good. And you don't have to make that bechamel sauce that all the English websites recommend but is a right old faff to make. In my recipe below, I've tried to make it as easy as possible, so every short-cut you can make is included. This lasagne still tastes amazing though, so give it a go.

Why is this any good?
Well, it uses a shop-bought lasagne sauce, so it's all ready to go. Buy your favourite one.

The lasagne sheets cook in the heat of the oven you don't need to part-boil them or anything. It's important that you cover the lasagne sheets completely with the sauce, otherwise you'll probably get a dry corner which means that bit will be crunchy and un-cooked. That's happened to me before and I was really pissed off about it.

Once you've cooked your lasagne, don't dig into it straight away, let it settle for about fifteen minutes and believe me, it will taste better. You can also make this lasagne the day before you need it and stick it in the fridge and then re-heat it when you're ready. It tastes GREAT the next day!

INGREDIENTS
- 1 onion
- 1 tablespoon of oil. Vegetable oil is fine. If you want to be all continental, then use olive oil instead. But have you seen the price of it? It's more expensive than cocaine according to my friend Mal who has thirty years of experience as a drugs mule.
- 1 pound of minced beef
- 1/2 teaspoon of salt, a couple of twists of black pepper
- 1/2(24 to 25-ounce) jar marinara sauce (or lasagne sauce as it's called in a lot of the UK supermarkets).
- A jar of white lasagne sauce from the supermarket. You may actually need 2 of these jars.
- 15 dry lasagne sheets (not no-boil, about 2/3 of a box)
- A block of your favourite cheese, grated.

Let's make it!
- Heat 1 tablespoon of oil in a frying pan or wok and heat until shimmering. Add the onion, the minced beef, the salt and black pepper, and cook. Make sure you break up the beef up into small pieces I use a wooden spoon. It should take about 8 minutes or so to cook the beef, then remove the pan and let it all cool for five minutes.
- Get a good-sized baking dish ready. (I use one which is 9x13 inches, roughly). Now open the tomato (marinara) sauce and mix it in with the beef you've just cooked.

Parmesan & Cream Cheese Pasta Sauce

This is a delicious sauce that you can use with things such as chicken or just vegetables if you want to go meat-free for a change… I originally saw this on an American recipe website, I tried it, and it blew me away. This is fantastic. Say what you like about the Americans, but they know how to make a quality sauce.

Ingredients:

- 8 ounces of cream cheese or soft cheese such as Philadelphia.
- ¾ cup of milk. I use semi-skimmed.
- 50g cup parmesan cheese
- A pinch of ground nutmeg (1/8 teaspoon, which is not a lot).
- Pepper (to taste).
- Garlic powder (Just a little bit).
- Olive oil just a splash.

How do I make it?

1. Good question. Microwave the cream cheese, milk and Parmesan cheese in a decent-sized microwaveable bowl until the sauce is nice and smooth, stirring occasionally.
   Then stir in the other stuff.
2. When it's ready, add it to some fresh pasta. A quick way to add chicken is to buy some already cooked from the supermarket.

This is the sort of look you'll get when you taste this lovely sauce…

Quick Q&A

Q: Am I allowed to dip my finger in the sauce in order to taste it?
A: Yes, as long as your finger hasn't been up you are. In which case the answer would be a firm "No".

Q: I don't actually like chicken, but I quite like turkey. Can I use that instead?
A: No, not unless it's Christmas.

Q: I suspect my wife is having an affair with the fella from number 67 with the flashy car outside. I don't feel like I should make this lovely sauce for her at the moment until our marital issues are resolved. What do you think?
A: I actually live at number 67 and she's moving in with me.

Chicken in Stilton Sauce

Now before you start saying, "Aw, I'm not interested in that smelly crap" just listen. Stilton sauce is a versatile sauce that you can use with all sorts of things such as steak, pork or chicken. It's really tasty, as well. And the important thing is, it's a doddle to make.

The description below is for the sauce. Cook your chicken and then make this sauce.

What will you need?

- 1 tsp butter.
- 1/2 small onion finely chopped if you can be arsed.
- 1 clove garlic peeled and chopped up into very small bits but you don't have to use garlic if you don't want to.
- 60 ml double cream.
- 50g Stilton cheese. Break it up into small pieces. You can use any blue cheese.
- 1 splash milk (optional).
- 1 squeeze of lemon juice (optional).
- Salt and pepper.

You've got the stuff, but how do you make it?

1. Melt the butter in a frying pan. Then add the onion and garlic with a pinch of salt until it starts to go a golden colour.
2. Now turn down the heat and add the cream and stilton which you've broken into small pieces already.
3. Keep stirring until the cheese has melted.
4. You can add a splash of milk and a squeeze of lemon if you want to. And don't forget the salt and pepper.
5. That's it – just pour it over your chicken or meat dish and proceed to wolf it down.

Notes

Prepare in advance and then reheat. Add milk to thin the sauce a bit if required.

Easy option

If you really can't be bothered messing around with ingredient, there's a simple way to make this sauce. Just get some stilton cheese and some single or double cream. Put the cream in a pan, heat it up and sprinkle the stilton cheese into it and keep stirring it. Hey presto, it's done. Add salt and pepper to taste.

What do you serve it with?

Well, chicken in stilton sauce is very nice with rice, pasta or new potatoes and vegetables. It's the sauce fir any occasion and is enjoyed by working class people like me these days, not just posh people. It really is a versatile treat for everyone (apart from my friend Roy who doesn't like stilton).

Dead Easy Macaroni Cheesy

This macaroni cheese recipe is so good, I'll be surprised if you don't have an orgasm while eating it! It's lovely and crispy on top, soaked in delicious sauce and is an absolute doddle to make. It should take you about 10 minutes to make unless you're an absolute moron, in which case, it can take anything up to 35 hours.

The recipe below should be enough for four people. Calories somewhere between 5 and 600, but does it really matter FFS?

You'll need:
- 300 g of macaroni
- 35 g of butter
- 25 g plain flour
- 500 ml of white milk
- 1 tsp mustard (or none at all it depends what mood you're in)
- 200g of cheddar cheese, grated. Mature is best for this, but anything you need to use up will also suffice
- Add salt and pepper

Instructions:
1. Preheat the oven to 220C / 200C Fan / Gas Mark 7. More or less.
2. Cook the macaroni first, until it's 'nearly' done. You know what I mean! Knock off a couple of minutes from what the instructions say.
3. While the macaronie is on the hob, don't wander off to watch Corrie or Emmerdale get on with the fucking sauce! Time management is the key.
4. Melt the butter on a low heat and then when the butter is foaming, mix in the flour. Keep stirring for a couple of minutes and everything will be alright.
5. Very slowly add the milk and don't forget to keep stirring. Do this slowly, on a low heat and gently stir don't go beserk. Seduce it! If you do this properly, you'll end up a lovely and smooth cheese sauce with zero lumps. If you fuck up, use a whisk to make it smoother, but I honestly have total faith in you. And I don't even know you!

Tip
Have some garlic bread with it. Why not push the boat out?

6. When all the milk is stirred in, add the mustard if you decide to add it. Now you should add half of the grated cheese and stir well. Then you can turn off the heat as you don't need it on anymore.
7. When the pasta is almost cooked as described before, you can drain it, and keep a little bit of the cooking water it was in.
8. Now tip all the pasta and two tablespoons of the cooking water into the cheese sauce and proceed to stir it in. Once you've done that, pour it all into an ovenproof dish and scatter the rest of the cheese over it.
9. That is pretty much it, you just need to bake in your oven for ten minutes or so when the top is brown and crispy, it'll be about ready.
10. Finally, dish up and eat.
11. If you want to make bigger portions next time, just double everything.

Recommended viewing while eating your macaroni cheese:
Casualty or Holby City
A light-hearted panel show starring Lee Mack
A period drama of some kind

Celebrities who might like macaroni cheese:
Football pundit Roy Keane, Graham Norton, and Antony Costa of the boyband 'Blue'.

Really Easy Spag Bol

Spag bol is a traditional British favourite, which was probably invented in Italy or somewhere like that. It does sound Italian, doesn't it? Anyhow, this is another meal which is not very difficult to make and is especially popular at mealtimes.

Ingredients
- A pack of minced beef
- A full pack of your favourite spaghetti
- A box of passata (tomato sauce) or jar of spag bol sauce
- Some garlic granules
- An onion
- Tin of chopped tomatoes
- Some tomato purees
- Some mushrooms

Method
1. Cut up the onion into small pieces. Oh, and don't forget to peel it first, your arsehole.
2. Then fry it in some vegetable oil and then add the minced beef until it's cooked. Then bung in the mushrooms until they're cooked nicely. Add some garlic granules and then pour in the tinned tomatoes. Open the tin first or you'll be waiting all night. Once you've done that, add a few squirts of tomato puree and the passata.
3. Then keep it simmering for ten or fifteen minutes.
4. At this point, get your water boiling for the spaghetti. Once you've added the spaghetti, it will take 10 or twelve minutes – but look at the packet just to check. I don't want people slagging me off online just because I gave you some shit advice.
5. Once the pasta is ready, you have to drain it, and then tip it into the sauce and mix it all together.
6. Some people like to serve the spaghetti and then put the sauce on top without mixing it in. It's up to you how you serve it up.

Interesting fact
When the US serial killer Jeffrey Dahmer was asked what he wanted for his final meal, he said 'spag bol'. They mustn't have cooked the minced beef properly though because he was dead within an hour of eating it.

The author (left) with his best pal Trevor having one of their 'dress a like twat' evenings. The outfits are available from Primark for £2.99

Piss-easy Carbonara

Ready in twenty minutes, or even less.
This is one of favourite and most popular recipes. Over 600,000 people voted it as their all-time favourite recipe in a dream I once had!
Actually, this is a very authentic carbonara and it really is simple to make whether you're sober or totally pissed.

What will you need?
- A packet of pecorino cheese (50g)
- A packet of parmesan or gran padano cheese (50g)
- 4 medium eggs
- A packet of smoked back (thin cut)
- Some garlic powder
- A packet of spaghetti
- Salt and pepper

How do you make it?
1. I always fry the bacon and get it nice and crispy first, then cut it up into small piece which will be sprinkled into the carbonara later.
2. Put the eggs into a bowl and add all the parmesan and two-thirds of the pecorino cheese with a bit of salt and pepper.
3. Boil some water in a pan and add the whole packet of spaghetti and cook until it's ready.
4. Once the pasta is ready and has been drained, pour the egg and cheese mixture into the pasta and make sure you mix it all in straight away. This is really important, or the mixture will 'curdle' and go all lumpy. So have two utensils ready to mix it all in. Once it's thoroughly mixed, add all the bacon and some salt, pepper and a pinch or two of garlic powder and mix it all again. Then it's ready to serve.
5. Finally, sprinkle over the pecorino cheese you saved at the start, add some salt and black pepper and tuck into your feast. If ever I go on to Masterchef, this is what I'll make as my signature dish. And not a fucking tuile in sight, whatever that is.

Can you have garlic bread with it?
You certainly can. And a great way of making easy garlic bread is to use a couple of flour tortillas.
Spread a little bit of butter on the first tortilla, then add grated cheese and some garlic powder. Then put another tortilla on top, spread a little butter and add grated cheese and a sprinkling of garlic powder and some salt and pepper.
Then stick it in the oven for five few minutes until the cheese is bubbling and brown. It really is dead simple to make and a very quick way to make delicious garlic bread. No skill required just how I like it.

The best music to listen to whilst making spaghetti carbonara according to industry experts is:
Dire Straits, Lana Del Rey or Kylie Minogue.

Interesting story...
My favourite restaurant made the best carbonara ever. I once took a potential girlfriend there and everything was going really well until she found a condom in here soup. And to make matters worse, the waiter was still wearing it!

Pizza Time

Have you ever watched people trying to make their own pizzas? What a performance, honestly. And let's face it, they all turn out to be shit, don't they? I've never been able to figure out why you'd try and make your own when you can buy them for a couple of quid from the supermarket.

So, this is how to have a lovely meal consisting of pizza. Firstly, if you've got enough money, ring Dominoes and order your favourite pizza. Do not pay full price – they always have special offers available.

If you can't afford a Dominoes, then pop round to your local supermarket and buy the cheapest, shittiest pizza you can find in the frozen section. Yes, the base might taste like fucking out-of-date cardboard, but this is what you need to do to fix the problem: Simply drink loads of alcohol.

And when the pizza is nearly ready, bung some more cheese on top of it. Of course, there is a slight chance that you'll be so drunk you'll forget you've got a pizza in the oven, and you'll burn your house down. But it's a risk that's worth taking.

1. Buy a cheapo pizza
2. Put it in oven
3. Drink booze
4. Add more cheese
5. Call for the emergency services if your house or flat is on fire
6. Eat pizza

Tips

- Why not watch a movie while eating your pizza? A good movie to watch is Limitless starring Bradley Cooper.
- There will always be some crust that is too hard to eat, and many people have asked me what they should do with it. Well, if I'm round at someone else's house, I sneakily ram it down the back of the couch.

Quick Q&A

Q: Do they eat Hawaiian pizza in Hawaii?
A: Actually, yes, they do. Three times a day, with extra pineapple.

Q: Where do pizzas come from?
A: The freezer

Q: George Michael was said to be a huge pizza fan. Any idea what his favourite pizza was?
A: Apparently, he loved a 10-inch.

Top question sent in via social media:

"Do pizzas have to be round? After all, they come in a square box, don't they?"

This is a very good question, and I think the answer is that yes, they do have to be round, as this is to comply with the EU Pizza Directive of 1985. According to online experts, pizzas are round so that there's always a little bit of space at the corners of the box so you can add a bit of garlic butter in a little pot.

Quick Q&A

Q: How many sausages can you have with your mash?
A: According to the European Court of Human Rights, you should have either three, four or five sausages. Plus, between 60 and 85 peas.

Q: What are gravy granules made out of?
A: Gravy granules are a cocktail of deadly chemicals which are left-over from the manufacture of nuclear weapons. They are shipped in from Russia. The granules themselves won't actually kill you, but they may limit the number of healthy children you can have.

Q: Could I substitute normal sausages for some of those fancy ones such as pork and apple sausages?
A: Unfortunately, because of Brexit, the answer is no.

What should you wear whilst eating bangers and mash?

Well, we rang leading fashion designer Victoria Beckham, but she was out at Nando's. We suggest something casual, but which has a little bit of style like the gentlemen in the photo, even though you may think you look like a wanker.

The author (centre) when he was in a pop group called The Symbolics. But then 'Sym' left, and it just wasn't the same...

Bangers & Mash

This is a traditional favourite and has always been in my top ten meals of all-time. Bangers are sausages, and you'll also need some gravy for this meal. Some people also like having peas with bangers and mash but I don't think they're totally necessary.

Sausages: You can cook these in a frying pan with some cooking oil or grill them. It's easy… I always prick the sausages with a fork at the start of cooking so it lets all the fat seep out. At least that's what I think it is. After about 15 or 20 mins on a moderate heat your sausages will probably be done.

Mash: Peel your spuds and cook them in a pan of boiling water. When you can easily stick a knife into the potatoes, they're about ready. Then drain them. Next, add a splash of milk, and a slab of butter and mash it like fuck. Add some salt and pepper too. Keep adding a bit more milk or butter until you've got a lovely creamy soft mash. Don't add too much milk or your mash will become like soup. Add the milk and butter a bit at a time. And keep mashing it to get all the lumpy bits pulped. Mash it for a good five minutes. Some people like to add cream to make the perfect mash, but not everyone's made of money. *In the past, sometimes I've left the potatoes unpeeled, and it still makes lovely mash, but the skins won't mash properly. The choice is yours.

Instant mash
This is the stuff you just add either water or milk to, and it's ready once the kettle has boiled. I used to use this a lot when I was a lazy c*** of a student. I always added a bit of butter and some salt and pepper – and that did the trick. It's always good to have in the cupboard for a supper-time emergency. Instant mash is good with some Branston pickle. Try it.

Gravy: Use gravy granules and you can't go wrong! More info below.

Ideas: bangers and mash are good on bonfire night!

Which sausages are the best?
Well, you may already have your own favourite sausage, in which case, I suggest you stick with those. I have tried Heck sausages which I bought in Tesco and they were fucking delicious. And can I just add that I have not been paid to mention Heck sausages by the company – although I do expect to receive some "free samples" off them for doing so.

What music is best to listen to while making bangers and mash?
The Beatles (The Revolver album)
Bruce Springsteen (The River album)
The Killers (Hot Fuss album)
Anything by Neil Diamond

Gravy Granules
Gravy granules are perfect for bangers and mash. Just put some granules into a cup and pour some boiling water on them and stir until the consistency is just how you like it.

I like to pour the gravy around the base of a mountain of mash. I also like to stick my sausages into the mash at an angle, like the Beano comic characters do. This, of course, is entirely optional, but it really does make your bangers and mash taste better despite there being no research done on this by anyone.

Did you know?
Bangers & Mash were a favourite of Shakespeare, although we have no proof of that whatsoever.

Tuna Pasta Bake

Here's a student favourite that doesn't take too long to make. It's a perfect dish for those winter nights when you've had a shit day and need something to make you feel better. Perhaps you've just been rumbled using AI for your thesis or something like that. Anyhow, this will make you feel much better about dishonesty.

- 500g rigatoni or your favourite pasta. I like that really big pasta where the sauce can go inside to add a surprise… god, I sound like Rick bloody Stein, god help me.
- 50g butter
- 50g plain flour
- 600ml milk
- 250g strong, grated cheddar
- 2 x 160g cans tuna steak in spring water, drained
- A small can of sweetcorn, or some frozen sweetcorn

Method

1. Heat oven to 180C/fan 160C/gas 4.
2. Boil 600g rigatoni for 2 mins less time than what it says on the pack.
3. To make the sauce, melt 50g butter in a saucepan and stir in 50g plain flour.
4. Cook for 1 min, then gradually stir in 600ml milk to make a thick white sauce.
5. Remove from the heat and stir in all but a handful of the 250g grated cheddar.
6. Drain the pasta, mix with the white sauce, two 160g drained cans tuna and a 330g drained can of sweetcorn. You can add some fresh parsley if you want to go a bit upmarket, although it's really not necessary.
7. Now stick it into a baking dish and top with the rest of the grated cheddar.
8. Bake for 15-20 mins until the cheese on top is golden and browny. Then it's done.

Quick Q&A

Questions send in by real people via social media. Enough said!

Q: What is this dish good with?
A: It's good with a knife and fork (or spoon if you're not supposed to go near sharp objects).

Q: I don't actually like Tuna, so what do I do?
A: To be honest, you should have mentioned that before you started making this. I think you may have something wrong with you. I really mean it.

Q: Is it acceptable to eat tuna pasta back immediately before having sex?
A: Yes. But try not to eat it *during* sex. That's plain rude, that is.

What the fuck is Asparagus?

No one really knows what asparagus is, but I believe and I may be wrong it's the vegetable version of rhubarb only without the big leaves at the end, and it's probably shit in a pie. The plus side of asparagus is that it's a nice change to other boring veg such as peas or broccoli. I read online that asparagus is good for you.

A downside of asparagus is that it is more expensive than other stuff, so most of the time, I just think 'fuck it' and get something else. BUT now and again it's a nice treat, and it actually tastes really good and a bit different.

But how do you cook it?

I've tried several ways, and the way I'm going to tell you now is easily the best. I nicked this off Gordon Ramsey, who I am a fan of, because he says it how it is. I like his Kitchen Nightmare TV show where the families have always fallen out and the owner is a total wanker. Then Gordon puts him in his place in order to save his restaurant and his marriage. Gordon then gets his crew in, and they give the restaurant a bit of overhaul, before the staff make a right old mess of things on their opening night. It's brilliant if a little repetitive.

Firstly, trim the end opposite the pointy bit.

Then put a little bit of olive oil and a knob of butter into a frying pan and when it starts to bubble, put the asparagus in the pan. Keep on a lowish heat and keep turning them for a couple of minutes. Pretentiously sprinkle on some salt and pepper, and after a couple of minutes, grate some parmesan cheese over the asparagus. And that's it. It only takes 2-3 minutes to it cook like this. Doddle!

Asparagus is good with:
Some cheese on such as grana padano or parmesan. You can get both of these in pretty much any supermarket.

Asparagus is good if...
- You're trying to impress someone.
- You want to appear to be middle-class
- You have it with some salmon.

Fun Facts
- Asparagus can be quite expensive
- It makes your urine smell funny
- You can bend asparagus quite a bit before it snaps
- No one knows where it comes from, although I have a feeling it comes from an asparagus tree.

I advise that you listen to music by any of the following artists as you eat your asparagus:

The classic album by Jane Birkin & Serge Gainsbourg
Van Morrison
I've heard it said that Orchestral Manoeuvres in the Dark go with asparagus, but I'm not sold on the idea (yet)
The Bugsy Malone soundtrack
Marc Almond sings Jacques Brel

Where do you get this so-called 'asparagus' from?
Most supermarkets have it. Amusingly, they usually tie it in little bundles.

Burgers

Everyone loves a burger apart from those that don't but they are a great thing to make. I buy those burgers from Aldi called Frikadellen. Guess what you just microwave them for two minutes and they're perfect burgers.

This is how I make the perfect burger feast.

Firstly, go to Aldi and buy some Frikadellen burgers from the refrigerated section (NOT the frozen section). Oh, and get yourself some brioche buns at the same time. I have no idea how they make brioche buns but they last for about a month, so they're always good to have in the cupboard for those late-night 'munchy' emergencies.

I also recommend you get some of the processed cheese slices from Aldi. They'll be in the 'dangerous chemicals' section. They taste good though, even though each slice may shorten your life by up to three years, according to inline theorists. I wouldn't take any notice of those twats.

1. Stick 2 Frikadellen burgers in the microwave for 3 minutes
2. Then get two slices of cheese, plonk them on top of each burger and microwave them for about 10-15 seconds until they're nicely melted
3. Place the burgers with cheese on, into one burger bun (stacked), or into two burger buns
4. Add either ketchup, BBQ ketchup etc whatever's your favourite.
5. Eat

Honestly, this is the easiest and tastiest way to make burgers. If you want to 'poncify' your burgers, you could add a lettuce leaf. I personally suggest you never, ever put anything green in a burger bun.

Fun Facts

- Burgers have been featured in many movies!
- Frikadellen burgers contain: Pork, onion, egg, garlic, nutmeg, spices and lots more. Just in case you're wondering, I got these ingredients off the packet.
- Aldi's Frikadellen burgers are from Germany
- In Aldi, you are not allowed to buy more than 15 packets of them! I don't know why that is one of their rules, but if you go onto their website, that's what they say. And that's absolutely true, so don't call me liar!

Recommended:

If you can be arsed, this is a really good thing to do. Fry some bacon until it's nice and crispy, and stick that on top of your cheesy burger. I think smoked bacon is best, but you might think you know better, so do what the fuck you want.

Good news!

You can eat Frikadellen burgers hot or cold – they are already cooked when you buy them. Result!

MAIN COURSES

Over the following pages you'll find a variety of ideas for main meals which are perfect for those evenings when you can't be arsed to do anything that will take you longer than a trip to the toilet.

I've tried to keep everything as simple as possible because life's too short to fuck about with complicated stuff.

Romantic Food

If you need to make something good, for example – you may have been an absolute twat, and need to apologise, so you've decided to cook your boyfriend or girlfriend a romantic meal… then where on earth do you begin?

Firstly, I'd be tempted to splash out at M&S and pretend you've made it yourself. All you have to do is destroy any packaging etc, so it all looks legit. However, if you've decided that you really need to make it yourself, then here are some ideas that might work.

These ideas are not difficult to do:

- Chicken in tarragon sauce, with either green beans or asparagus, and perhaps a tinned new potato or two!

- Steak in a peppercorn sauce with veg (you can buy the sauce already made in the supermarket)

- Carbonara with garlic bread

- Pasta with homemade pesto and wild mushrooms and maybe garlic bread

All the above are pretty easy to make and you'll find most, if not all of them somewhere in this amazing book. If your 'other half' is not really into food, then do the M&S option if you want to impress, or just stump up for their favourite takeaway that's sure to win them over.

ALTERNATIVE…

If your heart is not really in the relationship, then don't waste time and money, simply tell them that they're not worth the trouble, and end the relationship. It may hurt a bit at the time, but you'll feel so much better the day after when you do your online banking.

Tips for making the evening go well…
- No going on to social media while you're eating.
- Avoid any food that includes pastry. Although, if you decide to win them over with a 'Greggs' that's quite acceptable.
- Don't feed any scraps to the dog while you're at the table.
- Turn off the TV. You cannot heal a relationship whilst The One Show is on.
- Wear something nice. If you're still in your work gear consisting of a boiler suit and hard helmet, then you've actually got something wrong with you. Especially if you're a teacher.

Music to listen to while eating your romantic meal:

1. Elton John. You really can't go wrong with the tubby troubadour - although it's probably best to steer clear of his hit record 'Saturday Night's Alright for Fighting.'

2. Neil Diamond – always a favourite! And there's that bonding moment during the chorus of 'Sweet Caroline.'

3. Ed Sheeran. Not 100% sure about this choice, but he seems to be quite popular with the younger crowd, despite being ginger.

4. Billy Joel. 'The Stranger' album is probably the best album of all-time. Perfect for all-things romantic.

*Avoid playing any music featuring Coldplay.

Which Oil?

Let's look at the basics. There's olive oil and then there's vegetable oil. I can't think of anything else. Oh, hang on, there's sunflower oil.

Olive oil (and extra virgin olive oil) is good if you're sticking it on a salad, in a salad dressing or on roast potatoes. It's supposed to be better for you than the other oils. They use it a lot in Europe, and they say people there can live to be 187. But what's their quality of life? See what I mean? If they're just lying in bed in their own shite, then they're welcome to it.

What I do know is that olive oil is crap if you're doing a fry up. It makes your eggs taste awful. Don't let it near your full-English.

For basic frying, vegetable or sunflower oil is fine. So, anything that goes in a frying pan, basically. You can also just use butter for things like mushrooms. Or if you've run out of oil.

It costs a bomb

I have no idea why olive oil is so expensive. Let's say that it has to be collected from oil trees and then all the olives have to be squashed or something. So what? sunflower oil has to be collected from the veins of sunflower stalks doesn't it? Well, that can't be easy, yet it's much cheaper than olive oil. It makes no sense.

Did you know?
If you spill oil on the floor, it's quite possible you could slip on it and breaking your fucking neck!

Salad. Is it any good?

Let's think about salad for a minute. Is it really good for you? I actually don't think it is, and in fact, my mate Barry reckons it's the cause of most heart attacks. He could be right. My old next-door neighbour Trevor almost had a heart attack when he saw 2 gherkins in his Big Mac meal.

Many experts have said in the past that salad and vegetables are good for you but where is the proof? Exactly.

If you're one of those people who like salad, then I would suggest you put some of it next to some of the dishes within this book.

You may be surprised to hear that I actually like some salad things for example I love beetroot and I also love onions. And I think it's quite nice in the summer, for some reason. Anyway, who am I to tell you what to eat, just do what you want.

Quick Q&A

Questions sent in via social media from real people.

Q: Where does salad come from?
A: Just inside the door of Tesco, Asda, Sainsburys, Aldi and others.

Q: I'd like to put some salad in a sandwich. If I'm being specific, I'd say with some ham. Is this allowable under European law?
A: I am not sure about this, as we are no longer a part of the EU. I suggest you get in touch with the Citizen's Advice Bureau. It's a free service and they always have a legal expert on hand who is a salad specialist.

The author peeling some onions while his friend Roy watches, offering advice here and there. He's a fucking know-all, is Roy.

Garlic Mayo

This is the perfect thing to dip your oven chips in. There are lots of complicated ways to make garlic mayo but we're not going to bother with them as they end up costing you more than you want to spend. I looked at several recipes online and they used stuff like rapeseed oil – for fuck's sake, what's that all about? I think that was on the BBC website – typical of those twats – they think everyone is a civil servant on 50K plus a year.

Here's the best way to make garlic mayo and it won't break the bank.

1. Go and buy some mayo. If you're gluten free, you can buy that in most supermarkets, so it's no big deal.
2. Buy some garlic bulbs. You'll find these in the veg section at the supermarket. You can buy them separately, or there's usually about three garlic bulbs in a little bag for around a quid…

Ok, so you've now got all the ingredients. This is what you do!

Take 3 garlic cloves (that's the little segments like an orange) once you open a garlic bulb. Cut the rough ends off and peel them. Then chop them up into tiny pieces. Be careful if you're using a sharp knife or you'll have your fucking finger off. If this happens, proceed to A&E. But take a sleeping bag with you as you could be waiting for a fortnight in a corridor. Anyhow, you probably won't cut your finger off, so don't panic.

Next, get about 225grams worth of mayo from the jar you've bought and stick it in a bowl. Then tip in the garlic and give it a stir. Then have a taste of it. If it's too garlicky, add more mayo. Or if it's not garlicky enough, cut up another clove and add that. Also add a pinch of salt. I suggest you do it like the top chefs do- they bend slightly and hold their hand really high over the bowl and add the salt dramatically, as if you're an artist or something. Honestly, they are so fucking pretentious those chefs.

Then stick your garlic mayo in the fridge and you're all set.

Quick Q&A:
Q: Is garlic good for you?
A: "Yes!" according to my next-door neighbour Roy and he should know, as he once worked in a café.

Q: Can you choke on garlic?
A: Yes, if you try and swallow a whole garlic bulb. So best not to try.

Q: How much garlic mayo should you put on each chip?
A: Just enough to make it taste nice

Celebrity garlic lovers could include: The original James T. Kirk - William Shatner, singer Ellie Goulding, and rapper Snoop Dogg.

Celebrities who may not like garlic could include: Drake and Nicole Kidman.

Garlic Butter

This is one of the best things on the planet – it's on a par with McDonald's breakfast McMuffins and fish and chips. There are loads of ways to make garlic butter, but I prefer to keep it dead simple. Why the fuck would you spend twenty minutes making something you can make if five? Exactly.

For my garlic butter you need just three ingredients. I'm not counting the bread that you'll put it on.

What stuff do you need?

- 2 ciabatta loaves or some sliced sourdough bread
- 140g butter (nice and soft)
- 4-6 garlic cloves. Peel them, take off the crappy end bits and cut them up finely
- 2 tbsp finely grated Parmesan cheese

How to soften up your butter

If you're in a bit of a rush, then the quickest way to make butter soft is stick it in the microwave for 5 seconds at a time until it's soft. Don't stick it in for a minute or anything like that, or it'll go all runny and you'll have to throw it away.

1. Slice the bread in half lengthwise if you've decided to use ciabatta. Toast the crust side under the grill until really crispy. Mix together butter and garlic in a bowl. Spread over the bread and then sprinkle over the Parmesan.
2. Just before serving place under the grill for a few minutes. Let it cool for a minute and then cut up into smaller slices.
3. To store it, put it in the fridge in an airtight container.

If you're a parsley fan, you can add a bit during the process. If you don't want to add any parmesan to your garlic butter, then don't.

The green bits are parsley cut into tiny pieces. I never use parsley, cos I don't even know what it is.

Did you know?

Garlic is said to be very healthy for you in hundreds of different ways. I can't actually think of any of them off hand, but I bet if you look on Google, there'll be all sorts of stuff.

It's well-known that vampires don't like garlic. So, if you're friends with one, don't bother taking them to an Italian restaurant cos they'll fucking hate it.

Garlic can make your breath smell, so if you're planning a romantic evening where kissing (with or without tongues) may be involved, be careful with your menu choices.

Did you know?

You can also freeze pesto. Some people put their pesto into the compartments of an ice-cube tray, but I think that's a stupid idea. Imagine if your boss comes round and you make him or her a Baileys and add a pesto ice cube by mistake. Kiss your career goodbye.

How to make your own Pesto

Now, as much as I love Nigella, she does tend to fuck about in the kitchen, making a drama out of the simplest things. Did you see her making toast? Jesus, you'd think she'd just personally cooked a 12-course dinner for a thousand guests. Get a grip Nigella – it's just fuckin' toast.

Fresh pesto is so much better than you'll get in those jars in the supermarket, although in Aldi, they only cost about one-fifty, so you can't really go wrong with that. And they are pretty good, to be fair.

As a little treat every now and again, I'll make my own pesto, even though when I buy the pine nuts, I feel like I'm being robbed. This is how I make Pesto…

You'll need:
- 50g pine nuts
- Some basil (either a large fresh basil plant from the supermarket, or 2 of those little packets they have near the fruit and veg).
- 50g parmesan or gran padano
- 120ml olive oil
- 2 garlic cloves

Quick Q&A

Q: Does pesto last very long?
A: It will last four or five days in the fridge easily, but you can also stick it in the freezer and bring it out when you're ready. I've seen people say that it's worth putting the pesto into an ice-cube tray, and that way, you can just use however many cubes you want, rather than defrosting the whole lot and possibly wasting some… I actually said earlier that I don't like this idea, and I haven't changed my mind.

Q: Are there any other good uses for pesto?
A: Funny you should ask that. Yes, you can spread some on your bread if you're making a chicken sandwich and it's delicious. It's also great on top of cheese on toast.

How to make it:

1. Heat a small frying pan over a low heat. Cook the pine nuts until golden, shaking occasionally. This will take about a minute or even less. Put into a food processor with all the other ingredients and process until it's smooth, then add some salt and pepper. Taste it and then you can add more of individual ingredients until you're happy with it.

   If you want to go all 'Jamie Oliver' (and why would you?) then put a dash of lemon juice in and pretend you're a fucking Michelin star chef. To be honest, it does make it taste nice though, so respect to Jamie, even though he can be pretty annoying. Have you seen that exaggerated way he adds salt FFS!

2. Pour the pesto into a jar or Chinese takeaway container and cover with a little bit of extra oil, then seal and store in the fridge. It will keep in a fridge for about a week.

   Pesto is great with fresh pasta (or the non-fresh stuff). Bung in some chicken, mushrooms etc – after you've cooked them, obviously – and you have a delicious meal. Great to have some garlic bread with it too!

Tip: Make a cheese sandwich and spread some pesto on your bread. It tastes brilliant.

Celebrities who we think would like pesto include:
Bond villain, I can't remember his name, but I'm thinking of the guy who played Freddy Mercury in the Queen movie you know who I mean, don't you? Also, artist David Hockney and lead singer of the Sex Pistols, Johnny Rotten.

How to keep things fresh

There are two things that you need that will really help you to keep things fresh in the kitchen. The first is a roll of kitchen foil, the second is a roll of cling-film.

Foil

This is good for wrapping things like cheese in, after you've opened it and used a bit. Tear off some foil and wrap it, it keeps it really fresh. Of course, foil is not very effective if you are looking to re-cycle things and help the environment. In fact, I would go so far as to say that it's really shit for the environment. And I'm not even an expert in that area.

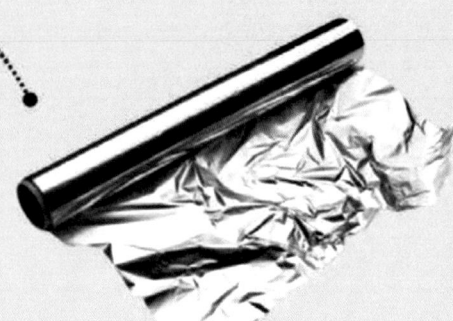

Clingfilm

This can be really annoying as sometimes you can't find the edge of the cling-film and then it rips and you can't find where the start of the cling-film actually is. And holding it up to the light makes no sense whatsoever. When this happens, I tend to swear a lot and then throw it in to the fucking bin. Sorted.

Chinese takeaway plastic containers

When you've finished a Chinese takeaway, why not save the plastic container it usually comes in and then re-use them? They help keep things fresh. FYI, my favourite Chinese takeaway (from The Mulan, just at the end of our road) is either chicken fried rice or Singapore noodles with vermicelli.

How to cook rice

That rice you buy in microwave packets is shit! Actually, that's a bit harsh because I've tried a packet coconut rice from Tesco and it's really good, so maybe I've been a bit hasty to slag it off. Some of it is good. And it's definitely convenient if you're in a rush, so the choice is yours.

Making your own basmati rice is best in my opinion, and here's the best way to make it...

1. Boil some water in a pan
2. Pour some rice (basmati is best) into the pan and make sure the water is covering all of it
3. Bring to boil and simmer
4. The rice is ready when you try it and it tastes nice and soft (usually about 10 mins)
5. Do not let the water boil away or you'll burn your rice
6. Put rice into a cullender (pan with little holes in) and pour some boiling water over it. This gets rid of the gungy, gooey stuff. I'm not sure what that stuff even is

Then put your rice onto your plate or into your bowl. Proceed to eat, with whatever you add to it. It could be a chilli or a curry.

Celebrities who possibly like rice include: Funny football pundit Ian Wright, cool pop legend Adam Ant, and annoying singer, Adele.

Research has shown that the best music to listen to while cooking rice includes:
I Shot the Sherriff by Bob Marley
It Doesn't Bother Me by The Distractions
Down in the Tubestation at Midnight by The Jam
I'm not getting excited by The Beths

Foodie Fact
Rice was invented by Pat Rice, who played for Arsenal in the 1970. This may not be true, but I tell everybody that it is.

The author sitting on a lady whilst waiting for his rice to cook.

Popular Q&As about Rice

Q: Why is rice white?
A: No one knows

Q: Is it acceptable to have sex whilst the rice is cooking?
A: Yes, as long as it doesn't distract the waiters in the restaurant

Q: Is rice good for you?
A: Yes, it's better for you than chocolate is, I'm pretty sure about that

Q: How much does rice cost per grain?
A: That's a fucking stupid question, so I'm not going to answer it. But if I was to answer it, I'd say each grain of rice cost about a tiny fraction of a penny. Maybe even less than that.

Top pasta tip

Don't forget to add salt and black pepper before eating. Plus, adding some grated cheese over the top of pasta is highly recommended, unless you don't like cheese, and then I wouldn't recommend it. Pecorino cheese is fantastic on top of pasta meals.

How to Cook Pasta

I know what you're thinking, "any tosser can cook pasta!" And, you're right! But this book all about doing things from scratch, so I'm going to go through this and make sure the message gets through.

Pasta is good for all sorts of meals. Stick some tomato sauce on it, and you have a basic meal. Stick some peas in it along with some meatballs and you've got a delicious, dead-easy tea. (Or 'dinner' if you're middle-class).

Fresh Pasta

Fresh past in the supermarkets is more expensive than the dried stuff, but I think it tastes better. It's definitely softer when it's cooked, so it's worth a try if you're feeling flush! Usually, you have to stick it in some boiling water for 3 or 4 minutes, drain it and it's ready.

Dried Pasta

Boil some water in a pan. Then turn the heat down so it's not sloshing all over the top of your fucking oven. If it does that, it's a nightmare. Now pour in some pasta shells… or, if you're doing spaghetti, the best thing to do is break the spaghetti in half and drop it into the water. That's deffo the easiest way of getting started. Usually, dried pasta takes about 10 minutes or so to cook through. Test it by having a taste. When it's nice and soft, it's done. Drain your pasta in a sieve and you're ready to do something with it.

Here are some things you can do with cooked pasta…

Pesto & Pasta

Get a jar of pesto and put some in with your pasta. Stir it around for a bit. Also, adding peas or sweetcorn is also a really good idea. Now, I don't expect for one minute that you have any pine nuts in your kitchen cupboard, but if you do, they are perfect sprinkled on top of your pasta. A good idea with pine nuts is to pour some into a frying pan without any oil for a minute and 'toast' them so they are a little bit brown. Then they're ready to sprinkle on your pasta.

*Red pesto or green pesto will be perfect!

Buy a bottle of sauce such as tomato and mascarpone (tomato & cheese). Add peas and you have a masterpiece. Obviously, I'm exaggerating a bit, but it's an easy, quick meal that only takes ten minutes.

Chicken & Pasta

Buy some pre-cooked chicken, cut it up and throw it in with your pasta and tomato sauce (once your pasta is done and ready) – or if you prefer something creamier, you can buy a ready-made mushroom sauce in the supermarket. Add salt and pepper and you're sorted.

Recommended music listening while cooking your pasta:

Sixties and seventies classic folk-pop with Simon & Garfunkel.

Take a trip to funks Ville with Bruno Mars.

Pasta time is Bowie time!

Popular Q&A's

Q: Why do they make pasta is lots of different shapes and colours?
A: Who gives a fuck?
Q: What do they use to make pasta?
A: Google it.
Q: Is it possible to have pasta AND chips on the same plate?
A: Yes, as long as your plate's big enough.
Q: if you are testing the pasta and drop a piece on the floor, can you put it back in the pan?
A: Yes – but only if no-one notices.
Q: Are there any other uses for pasta?
A: Yes, they sometimes use pasta in schools to stick on art collages in classes for very young children especially near Xmas time.

HOW TO...

In the following section, I will be revealing how you do stuff.

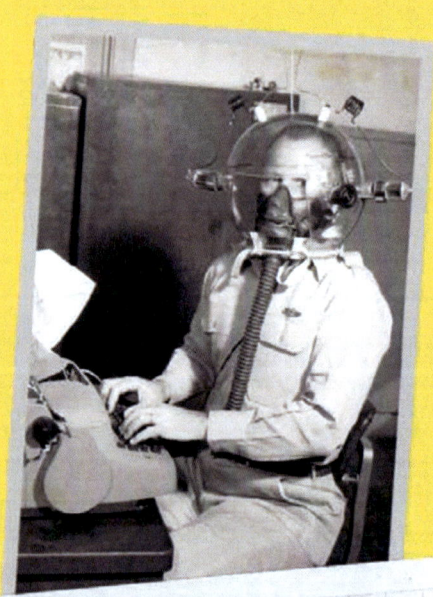

The author writing this book whilst practicing for a forthcoming party for sexual deviants

Kitchen Utensil Management

What does 'kitchen utensil management' actually mean? Well, how many times have you been looking for a big spoon or something like that in all the drawers and cupboards, and it's driven you up the flamin' wall? Well, this won't be a problem in future if you follow my professional advice.

The answer is very simple: Throw everything you have into one big box. Then, whatever it is you're looking for, you know it's in that box. I'm surprised all the top restaurants in London don't do this, as it makes total sense.

Here are my views on some of the implements you might think about using in the kitchen:

Potato Peeler

This little gadget seems pretty nifty, but I prefer to use a knife to peel potatoes. I've used the gadget a few times and I find that it can't get into those nooks and crannies that potatoes have. You know what I mean don't you? A knife does away with the confusion. I accept that the peel will be thicker, but who really gives a fuck? Not me. I've got more important things to worry about.

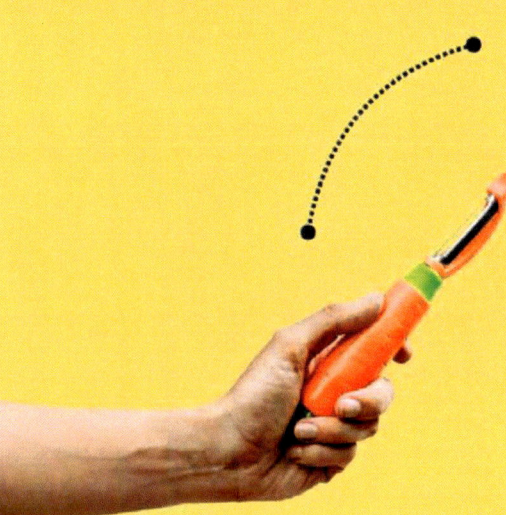

A tray

These metal trays are a godsend if you want to put some oven chips in. They are so versatile – you can put other things on them too, like Chicken Kievs and sausages. In fact, you can put anything on them that will fit.

You can never have enough baking trays in my opinion. One is definitely not enough. If you don't have enough trays, you'll get really stressed out and then you may lose your temper and say things like, "why the chuff have I only got one baking tray when I need two?" So, you see, it's best to have two. Or even three.

The Perfect Cheese on Toast

So, you've just got in at 4am and you need something substantial before hitting the floor! Cheese on toast is a traditional favourite with students, as it's easy to make and cheap. Plus, if you're eating it at 4am you really don't give a fuck what it tastes like anyway. You've probably already had a kebab made out of old carpet slippers on the way home.

The key to good cheese on toast is to make sure one side is properly toasted, and then do the other side so it's like half toasted. Then put some butter on and some slices of cheese on and then put it back under the grill until the cheese is bubbling nicely. Then – and this is up to you – put some ketchup on. DO NOT use the cheap Aldi shit. Use Heinz.

Let me just clarify that I'm from a working-class background, and I appreciate that saving money on food shopping is important. But. You must never scrimp on ketchup. And Heinz are not even paying me to say this.

Music artistes who are good to listen to while making cheese on toast:
Guns & Roses
Shania Twain
Dua Lipa
*Avoid Blossoms and Keane at all costs.

Quick Q&A:
Q: You mentioned kebabs earlier... What's actually in a kebab?
A: No one knows

Q: What sort of cheese is best to use for cheese on toast
A: Those square processed sheets of cheese are good, you know the ones that don't contain any cheese. They're probably made out of asbestos or something like that.

Q: How many slices of cheese on toast will suffice?
A: That depends on how full you get when eating them. No more than 23 slices is my golden rule.

Q: Can you eat cheese on toast in bed?
A: Yes. Cheese on toast is so versatile that you can also eat it when you are not in bed!

Q: If you drop a slice of cheese on toast on the floor, can you still eat it?
A: If you are drunk, definitely. Any excess fluff probably won't kill you.

Hot Dogs

Here's one of the world's greatest mysteries. No one, not even the makers know what exactly is in a hot dog sausage. All I can say for certain is that they've never been anywhere near meat. They could be made out of nuclear waste for all I know, but stick them in a bread bun with some fried onions and ketchup and they taste fucking awesome. And if you eat them outside on a chilly night, they taste even better.

Step-by-step guide:
1. Open tin
2. Tip hot dogs into boiling water (or microwave on their own if you're in a rush)
3. When they're really hot, they're done

Events which are suitable to have hot dogs at:
Bonfire night
Sports fixtures
Funerals

Events which are probably NOT great to eat hotdogs at:
Anti-hotdog gatherings
Chess competitions
Any events where royalty is present, such as the crowning of a monarch

The author (back) with his close friend Neil, about to indulge in some sausage-related fun.

Peanut Butter Sandwich

I used to think that peanut butter was just something that annoying American kids ate in movies. I know that they love 'peanut butter and jelly' sandwiches and jelly in America is actually what we call 'jam'. Anyway, I discovered peanut butter a few months ago as there was nothing else in my cupboard so I tried it. And you know what? It was fucking fantastic!

The key to a good peanut butter sandwich is to have it on cheap white bread. You know, the sort of bread that tests have shown to be of no nutritional value whatsoever. The sort of bread that if you squeeze it between your fingers resembles Blutac. But peanut butter tastes great on it. So, do not under any circumstances spread it on posh bread.

Elvis used to have peanut butter with bacon and sliced banana. And Elvis loved his food, so maybe that's worth a try too. Online, lots of people reckon salted crisps are fantastic in a sandwich with peanut butter. But then again, we know how many nutters are online.

I recommend you use crunchy peanut butter rather than the smooth stuff. And if you have a peanut allergy, I wouldn't bother with peanut butter sandwiches as they may contain nuts.

Tip
When placing your peanut butter in your cupboard, place it next to the baked beans, then you'll always know where it is!

Bread: Use white bread. It will probably help to kill you, but it's worth it!

Tip: Spread your peanut butter on thick, so it clogs your teeth up.

Music to listen to whilst eating your peanut butter sandwich: Alicia Keys, Adam & The Ants, Manic Street Preachers.

DO NOT listen to the following whilst eating a peanut butter sandwich: Duran Duran, Cliff Richard, Craig David.

For a poncy option my publisher suggests having peanut butter & jam on a crumpet so, I'm adding this in so she publishes the book...

A wok. I'm pretty sure I'm right this time.

A huge fly swatter.

A whisk. Perfect for things that need a whisk.

I don't know what you call these, but they are good for picking up your worn underwear and putting them in the wash.

More Tools!

As you rummage in your kitchen drawers, you might come across some of these. What are they? I'm not totally sure, but I'll have a guess!

A mini frying pan that is absolutely no use to anyone. C'mon. Honestly.

This is the Tesco 'kitchen tools' aisle. One of the most difficult aisles to shoplift from, according to my grandma.

A potato masher. Also used by drugs cartels in Hull to mash up lumpy cocaine, according to my probation officer.

I think this is for shaving men's facial stubble. Not sure.

This is a brush. I'm pretty definite about that.

Egg Mayo

You see these sandwiches 'ready-made' in your local supermarket and they are really tasty and very easy to make.

1. Boil 2 eggs in a pan. Let them have 7 or 8 minutes in simmering, boiling water.
2. Peel the shells off the eggs
3. Place the peeled eggs into a small bowl or dish
4. Add mayonnaise until it's the sort of consistency you like
5. Add salt and black pepper to taste

That's it. That wasn't difficult at all, was it? All you have to do then is put some of it between two slices of bread and the job is done.

If you make too much egg mayo, then you can put it into the fridge and it will last for a few days. Just either put some clingfilm over the dish or use some kitchen foil.

Some people like to add some cress to their egg mayo in a shit attempt to make it look like the sort of sandwich they sell in Marks and Spencers. I personally think that adding cress is for wankers. It gets stuck between your teeth and the health benefits of eating a bit of cress in any sort of sandwich is minimal, so why fucking bother?

Egg mayo is great for eating whilst watching the following movies:
Jaws
Downton Abbey (The Movie)
Spiderman starring Tobey Maguire

Do NOT eat egg mayo during the following movies or TV series:
Notting Hill starring Hugh Grant
The Walking Dead

Interesting Fact

Believe it or not, if you put crushed egg shells around your prized plants in the garden, it stops slugs from eating them, as they can't slither past the pieces of shell! Ha ha, that'll really piss them off!

Cheesy chips

I have never been a massive fan of cheesy chips for some reason. It's weird, because I love chips and I love cheese – but put them together and I'm not so enamoured. However, I know that cheesy chips are a go-to snack for those returning home from a night club at 5am, so I thought I'd have a little experiment and see what works the best.

Oven chips

These have really improved in recent years, and I'm pretty sure a lot of restaurants use frozen chips on their menu. The Tesco 'best range' or whatever it is, are brilliant. Crispy on the outside and nice and fluffy on the inside. Once they're more or less done, you need to put some grated cheese over the top of them. And some sea salt. You can't have chips, or cheesy chips without salt on. And maybe some vinegar.

If you want the best cheesy chips, stick the chips with cheese on under the grill for a couple of minutes until the cheese all bubbles. Yeah, I know it's a bit of a faff at 6am when you're pissed, and you'll probably set the house on fire, but the risk is worth it.

What sort of cheese is best?

I love those cheese slices that they sell in Aldi and other supermarkets. They melt really easily. Finish off by dipping them in ketchup as you eat them. Or better still, make a cheesy chips sarnie out of them.

Tip: BBQ sauce is great on cheesy chips. Ketchup is always good. And Peri-Peri salt is awesome.

Celebrities who I think would probably love cheesy chips include:

Hollywood superstar George Clooney, Australian Hugh Jackman and Rita Ora.

Did you know?

Cheesy chips are perfect for whilst watching a horror movie. But I don't recommend you eat cheesy chips when watching pornography. It's just not right. And it's probably not legal either.

Hot Meatball Sandwich

This is one of the easiest things to make. Get some meatballs from Aldi. The German-made frikadellan meatballs in Aldi are fantastic. They're already cooked, so you can just stick them in the microwave for a couple of minutes and you have perfect meatballs. Most supermarkets probably sell pre-cooked meatballs so have a look the next time you're in Tesco etc but the Aldi ones take some beating.

This sandwich is perfect when you come in after a night out and you've got the munchies. This takes about 2 minutes to make, which is awesome.

What do you need?
- 2 slices of white bread
- Butter or similar spread
- 6 meatballs
- Cheese
- Ketchup

How do you make it?
1. Toast your bread and then put some butter on it.
2. Take 6 meatballs and put them in a microwaveable dish and give them 2 minutes. Half-way through microwaving them, put some cheese over the top of the meatballs. Once they're hot, cut the meatballs in half and put them on the toast, and then either put some ketchup on them or BBQ sauce is also a winner. Put the other slice of toast on top, press down, cut in-half and you have an amazing supper snack.

What is a good movie to watch while eating your hot meatball sandwich?
Back to the Future II
50 Shades of Grey
E.T

Tip

Once you've eaten it, make another, cos they are incredible – especially when pissed. You don't have to toast the bread if you don't want to. Whatever.

- Perfect for eating in bed (but watch the ketchup)
- Perfect for day or night
- Perfect snack to impress a potential partner

Microwave 'grilled' cheese sandwich

For this, you'll need 2 slices of your favourite bread, a bit of butter and as much cheese as you want in your sandwich. Personally, I'd go for three cheese slices.

This is how you make it...

Firstly, toast your bread until it's just how you like it. Then put the butter on your toast as you would do normally. Then put the cheese between the two slices, along with anything else you're bunging in.

Now here's the clever bit. Wrap a moist piece of kitchen roll around your sandwich and stick it in the microwave for about 20 seconds. This kitchen roll keeps your toast in perfect condition. Clever, eh? I can't take credit for it though – I saw someone on Facebook doing it.

Did you know?

The microwave oven was invented by Barry Microwave who lives just outside Hull, although someone recently told me that he'd moved to London as his parents are very ill... and he didn't want to be near them,

TOP TIP:

Don't make your crisps sandwiches the night before, as they go all soggy overnight. I'm not actually sure if this is true, but I read it somewhere online.

Celebrities who might enjoy a crisp sandwich include:

Football manager Jose Maurinho, artist Grayson Perry, and cellist Julian Lloyd Webber.

Good movies to watch whilst eating your crisp sandwich

I tend to find that light-hearted movies are good whilst eating a crisp sandwich. Movies such as: There's Something About Mary, About Time, Meet the Parents, Bridesmaids and Mean Girls are all very good. Don't bother watching Blinded by The Light, as it's utter dogshit.

Quick Q&A

Q: How many crisp sandwiches should you eat in one sitting?
A: I personally eat two, and then usually go and get a biscuit

Q: Are supermarket 'own-label' crisps any good?
A: Yes, they are really good.

Q: What other crisp-like products work well in a sandwich?
A: Wotsits are very good. And so are pickled onion Monster Munch... I've never made a Quaver sandwich, but I bet those are tasty, too.

Crisp Sandwiches

Here's an underrated classic that's cheap, tasty and helps you beat the cost-of-living crisis. You can have one as a main meal if you have Having Guests Round, or simply have one as a bedtime treat. A crisp sandwich is super-versatile.

Many people struggle with picking the right flavour crisps to make their sandwich into a winner. Well, I've made loads of these, and the best crisps are Walker's cheese & onion. There's no comparison, and just in case you were wondering, I am not being paid by Walkers to say this. Primarily because they never answered my emails asking for sponsorship money.

Do not fall into the trap of thinking that those expensive crisps will be better for sandwiches just because they cost more. They are shit. And here's another tip don't even bother trying those poncy flavours like Rosemary & Thyme, or Balsamic vinegar and dogshit. NONE OF THEM WORK IN A CRISP SANDWICH.

A word of warning: ONLY USE SLICED WHITE BREAD WHEN MAKING A CRISP SANDWICH.

The only flavours which work in a sandwich are:
- Walker's cheese & onion
- Walker's smokey bacon flavour
- Seabrook cheese & onion or roast chicken flavour
- Walker's chicken flavour

*Some supermarket own brands are really good and are worth trying… but I would avoid any crisps which are 'ridged' as for some reason these are just not as good as the traditional crisp.

Fact

This was told to me by an industry 'insider'. Supermarket own-brand crisps use a better-quality potato and more flavour in their crisps! I'm only passing on what I was told.

How to make a crisp sandwich:
Preparation time: *48 seconds if everything is close by. If you can't find the butter, 4 minutes 67 seconds. If a chatty neighbour comes to the door: 1 hour and 16 minutes.*

1. Get 2 slices of thin or medium sliced WHITE bread.
2. Put some butter or cheap spread on the bread. Butter is always best. Now open your crisps and put in a fair amount. Now place one slice of bread on top of the other and press down firmly with your hands so that all the crisps break up and then stick in the butter or whatever it is you've used. Now here's the important bit: You must press hard enough so that you leave an imprint of your hand in the bread. The firmness of your press ensures that the crisps are 'stuck' into the bread and won't fall out as you eat your sandwich.
3. That's about it. It's not rocket science, but it does make a fantastic crisp sandwich. And a crisp sandwich is great with a cup of tea!

Fish Finger Sandwich

Who doesn't like a fishfinger sandwich? Well, my mate Brian who works in Tesco for a start – but that's not important. The fish finger sandwich is one of those things that make us all feel proud to be British. It's comforting, filling and has been a staple of the working-class diet since the fish finger was invented by Captain Birdseye back in the 1970's. The man was an absolute genius. But what sort of fish is inside the breadcrumb coating? No one really knows, but that's what creates the exotic intrigue. It could be cod, it could be haddock, or it could be all the left-over bits such as fish eyeballs and fish anuses. But it tastes good, so we don't give a fuck.

The Golden Rules...
- You MUST use white bread for your fishfinger sandwich
- Use tomato ketchup if at all possible
- When you've put the sandwich together, there has to be a ceremonial 'squashing down' of the bread, so you can see your palm print in it

To cook:
Either stick the required amount of fish fingers in the over for about 20 mins on 190 degrees or shove them into a frying pan with some vegetable oil and cook them for about 15 minutes or so. When they're hot all the way through, they're done.

Advice:
If you EVER see or hear of anyone putting lettuce in a fish finger sandwich, then you should immediately report them to the police. They need to feel the full weight of the law on top of them. Interestingly, in Russia, there is an automatic five-year prison sentence for anyone putting lettuce in a fish finger sandwich, but to be honest, there's an automatic five-year prison sentence for breathing in Russia.

Never put anything green next to your fish fingers

Quick Q&A
Q: What's the ideal length of a fish finger?
A: Just long enough

Q: Can you have more than one fish finger sandwich?
A: Yes, if you're hungry enough then it seems to make sense.

Famous people who love a fish finger sandwich could include:
President Putin, the absolute wanker who runs Russia
The drummer of Green Day
70's singer Gilbert O'Sullivan

"It's a Wrap!"

Easy stuff you can make by sticking it in a wrap… for all these super-quick treats you'll need to have a microwave oven. Most of these can made in 60 seconds.

Beans and Cheese

Firstly, stick a spoon-bull of beans (or two) on your open wrap, then sprinkle cheese on top. I use medium cheddar. Then put some black pepper and salt on, wrap it all up and stick the fucker into the microwave for about a minute. Then you have a lovely gooey mush of hot means and melted cheese. If you want to add something extra, then some crispy bacon works a treat. Obviously, you need to fry the bacon first.

Cheese & Onion

Simply put some cheese and raw onion together on an open wrap, add salt and pepper, fold up the wrap and give it a minute in your microwave. A bit of tomato ketchup (or BBQ sauce) in there as well gives it the great 'cheese-on-toast' taste!

Hot Doggedy-dog!

Here's a dead easy wrap to make. Stick a couple of hot dogs on to an open wrap, along with some ketchup and a bit of Dijon mustard if you want to be fancy. Fold-up the wrap and give it a minute in your microwave. Sorted!

Ultra-quick Vegetarian Mexican

Put some refried beans, kidney beans, cheese, salsa and guacamole on to your open wrap. Fold it and then microwave it. An easy Mexican wrap in a jiffy. Add a bit of sour cream too if you're that way inclined. Plus, don't forget the salt and black pepper. Result. This is so authentic that you'll feel like you're part of a Mexican drugs cartel.

Corned Beef

Many younger readers might never have heard of corned beef. This is another one of those food items that no one really knows what it contains, but it tastes amazing. Cut some corned beef and stick it on your open wrap. Add some Branston pickle and you've got a perfect snack.

Just in case you don't know where to get your corned beef from, you can either buy a tin of it from your local supermarket, or you can buy slices of it already cut. You'll usually find this next to the ham.

The wrap itself…
You can buy these from any supermarket

- and they say that wholemeal wraps are healthier for you.

Quick Q&A

Q: What are wraps made out of?
A: I'm not sure.

Q: Can you have some chips with your wrap?
A: Yes, that's actually not a bad idea.

Q: Can you add some salad into your wrap to make it a bit healthier?
A: Yes, I suppose you could.

Best movies or TV shows to watch while you're eating your wraps…

Ghostbusters (the original version, not the crap remakes).

Pet Semetary, the Stephen King horror movie. I don't know why Americans spell cemetary with 's', it makes no sense.

Any of the Indiana Jones movies.

TV series Breaking Bad.

Beans on toast

A true British classic. A heady combination of beans on some bread. A culinary masterpiece mixing a traditional favourite with… well, another traditional favourite. As His Majesty the King would say, "this is a piece of piss!" Let's deconstruct this all-time classic.

What do you need?
- Beans (tin)
- Bread (cheap white loaf)
- Butter or something pretending to be butter

Tools required
- A toaster
- Knife
- Spoon
- Pan or microwave

Go Upmarket
Why not go all middle-class and put some cheese on top?

To Make
Put beans into microwave. Turn it on. You'll know it's working as your beans will be spinning around inside. When they are hot, empty beans on to some toast that you have pre-buttered. Proceed to eat. Salt and pepper to taste.

Celebrities who might like this dish:
Danny Dyer, Dame Judi Dench, Judge Rinder.

Good with...
An episode of a soap opera such as Emmerdale or Corrie.

Tip

Do not wear a white shirt whilst eating it as beans tend to have a splatter-factor.

Banana Sandwich

This takes me back to my school days. After a hard day's smoking behind the bike sheds, I'd come home ready for a slap-up tea consisting of an over-ripe banana mushed-up on two slices of white bread. It was the perfect meal for the teenager who needed to eat fast before he went out causing trouble on an evening. Happy days.

For many kids growing up in the 60's, 70's and 80's a banana sandwich was almost a treat and they were especially popular during the summer holidays. Are they still popular today? Well, I guess on rough housing estates throughout the land they may well be a staple diet.

Banana sandwiches are cheap and nutritious… but how do you make one? Well, there are some very strict rules, so stray from them at your peril!

1. Use only SLICED, WHITE BREAD for banana sandwiches. Anything else is shit.

2. Do not EVER put butter on your bread first. The banana does all the work!

3. Mash the banana straight on to the bread and squash down with the palm of your hand. Don't cut the banana into little circular slices. The banana must be mashed with a fork straight on to the bread. It's this that gives it the perfect texture…

So there you have it. Making a banana sandwich is not difficult and it can be fun.

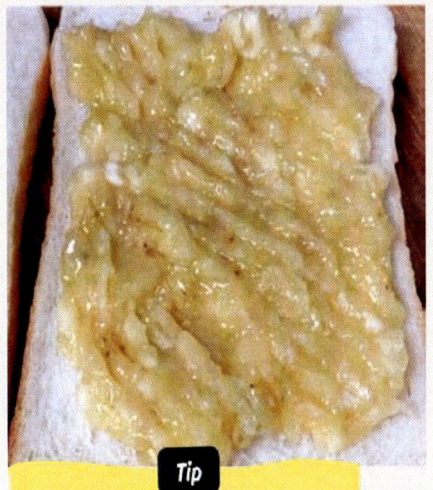

Tip

Make your banana sandwich and eat it then. Don't make it to eat several hours later as the banana will have gone all brown and squishy and the bread will have gone a bit mushy. That once happened to me when my mum gave me a banana sandwich to take on a school trip, and the whole day was ruined by it. I threw it away, but told my mum it was delicious.

Quick Q & A

Q: Who invented the banana sandwich?
A: We don't know.

Q: How many banana sandwiches can you eat before you start to feel a bit sick?
A: About four according the government sources.

Q: What size banana is best to use?
A: I find that anything between two and eleven inches will be perfect…

Q: Where is it best to buy bananas from?
A: A shop

A Greggs

OK, this is cheating a bit, but I'm including it just in case you can't be arsed to cook anything after a long day of watching daytime telly. I suggest you clutch a few quid and go and treat yourself to a bag of Greggs sausage rolls because they are awesome. What do they put in them to make them so addictive? I've never taken cocaine, but I would guess that a Greggs sausage role is the legal equivalent.

If I had the chance to make love to a Hollywood superstar or have a night in front of the telly munching on a bowl of Greggs sausage rolls, then I would have to go for the meaty treat. Unless of course it was Tom Cruise – who is actually a smaller meaty treat than a Greggs sausage roll as it turns out.

What you need:
A few quid and an empty stomach.

Quick Q & A

Q: Do you need to heat them up in the microwave?
A: No. Unless you need them warming up.

Q: How long is a Greggs sausage roll?
A: We're not sure, but from memory they are somewhere between 3 inches and 2 foot seven inches long.

Q: Any other Greggs food worth having?
A: Their pasties are good, and when you put them on a plate next to some oven chips, they look the business. Their cheese and onion pasties are especially good. But a word of caution: If you aren't careful, they can burn the roof of your mouth, like pizzas sometimes do.

Celebrities who we think would like Greggs sausage rolls: Footballer Tyrone Mings, ex-Olympic gymnast Olga Korbut, loudmouth Liam Gallagher and the ex-Archbishop of York John Sentamu.

Celebrities who we don't think would like Greggs sausage rolls include: Ex-A-ha's Morten Harket, law-flouter Richie Sunak and actor Ben Afleck.

Please note that Greggs have not paid me anything to promote their products – despite me emailing them thousands of times.

Snacks and Sarnies

From the classic crisp sandwich to the underrated beans on toast, here are some of the greatest-ever British recipes for those who can't be arsed to spend a single-second doing more than absolutely necessary in the kitchen.

A Healthy Breakfast

I can hardly bring myself to write anything here. Who really wants a breakfast consisting of a tiny pot of yoghurt with a slice of melon or something? That is not going to keep you going for the whole morning. That's the sort of thing that you'll eat and then as soon as you're out of the house, you'll be in the local shop for a pasty or a king size Mars Bar.

Take my advice: Fuck those so-called 'healthy' breakfasts because they're shit. I think I've made a convincing argument there.

Your Kitchen Dilemma

This is the bit where you tell us about a particular difficulty you are having in the kitchen and then Graham will tell you what you need to do to sort it out. He's a bit like an Agony Aunt of the Kitchen, although he's actually a man. Are we even allowed to say that these days? No, I didn't think so.

We received an interesting email from a gentleman called Liam Walker, who's name we will not reveal due to GDPR rules. Anyway, below is his email highlighting a problem. Graham then answers it below. It's quite easy to follow, even for someone who's on crystal meths.

I asked AI to produce a photo of a typical student fridge, with a BigMac in it, and this is what it produced. AI knows fuck all about students.

A kitchen sharing issue...

Hi, I share a house with some other students, and they keep stealing my food from the fridge, but when I ask them about it, they all deny it and say it was one of the others. Sometimes, I just want to poison them all. What should I do to sort out this sorry mess? And, while I'm talking, I also think they're stealing my class A drugs too. What should I do?

Graham replies: Well Liam, I fully understand your frustration. I have personal experience when it comes to drugs, as my 94-year-old grandma worked as a drugs mule for a Colombian drugs cartel but she was arrested at Heathrow airport and charged with carrying 2 ounces of cocaine in her handbag. They would've charged her with more, but no one was willing to do the strip search.

I suggest you get all your housemates together and hit them with a baseball bat until one of them cracks. If anyone calls the police, simply claim that you were only following your religious beliefs. That's literally your get-out-of-jail-free card. Result!

If you don't want to go down the gratuitous violence route, move out without paying your share of the bills. A little bit more debt won't harm them as, they'll all abe leaving uni with about 50K of debt anyway, so what's the big deal? Sorted.

Cereal - Why

Q: Is cereal worth bothering with?
A: No, not really.

Cereal is the sort of thing you tend to eat when you get up in the morning and can't be arsed to make anything else. I sometimes have some cereal at supper time if I'm still hungry before I toddle off to bed.

Here are some good ideas for when you have cereal:

1. Once you've poured out the cereal you want, into a bowl, make sure you seal the packet properly before you put the box of cereal away or it will go all soft and it will really piss you off the next time you want some.
2. You can add some things like blueberries and raisins if you want to make it a little bit healthier. Especially if you're having oats or porridge-type stuff.
3. To be honest, you'll feel much better if you just have a lovely crispy bacon sandwich instead. Fuck cereal!

Quick Q & A

Q: If you were being sponsored by Kellogs, would you have a much more favourable view of cereal
A: Yes, I definitely would.

Q: I heard somewhere that lots of cereals contain sugar, sort of hidden inside them somehow. Is that true?
A: I wouldn't put it past those crafty cereal companies to do that.

Waffles

Don't panic, I'm not going to suggest you make your own waffles, even though you've got a waffle-maker up in the attic somewhere. There's no need to go to so much trouble.

If you've ever been to America, you might have visited a Waffle House, where they make brilliant waffles. The way of recreating them here is by going into Aldi (or a different shop) and buying some Belgian sugar waffles. There are about 5 individually wrapped waffles for about a pound or something. They are really tasty, and all you have to do is stick them in the toaster.

When they're ready, pour some maple syrup on them and you're sorted. If you want to feel a bit healthier, then add some blueberries and strawberries. And if you want to feel more American, add some soft scoop ice cream and you've got an amazing breakfast, or whatever.

Idea!
I like to make a full English breakfast and stick a couple of waffles and maple syrup on it too. This is awesomely awesome.

Maple syrup
Genuine maple syrup (usually from Canada) is hard to beat, but Tesco do a fantastic alternative which is much cheaper and healthier. It tastes just as good in my opinion but it's about half the price.

Quick Q&A
Q: What are waffles made out of?
A: I don't know. Maybe eggs and something else?

Q: Are you likely to get shot if you visit America?
A: possibly.

Q: How many waffles will fill you up?
A: 2.17 waffles, according to the lady who cuts my hair.

Top tip
Keep your waffles in a cupboard until needed.

The author (left) and his pals in their favourite waffle outfits

TOAST

There's nothing better than a nice slice of toast. But you have to use proper butter, not that stuff that is trying to pretend to be butter. There is no substitute for real butter.

What you'll need:

- Toaster
- Butter
- Knife
- Bread

How do you do it?

Well, it's a little complicated, but please bear with me. Firstly, make sure the toaster is plugged in or you'll look like a prize twat an hour later when you go to check on the progress of your bread.

- Put 'raw' bread in toaster
- Wait for bread to pop up
- Put on butter

TOP TIP:

Make sure the butter has not been left in the fridge or it'll be too hard to use. If your butter is solid, you can cut a bit off and put it in the microwave for about ten seconds and it should be nice and spreadable. Lurpak do spreadable butter but it's quite expensive so you have to think about your cashflow situation before deciding.

Did you know?

Toast was invented by Terry Toaster from Uttoxeter in 1978, who discovered that when you burn bread and put butter on it, it is nice. Hence, the name 'toast', although according to Wikipedia it was the Romans who invented it. Sounds farfetched to me, as toasters weren't invented until recently – so how could they have invented it? It's bollocks, that.

Scrambled Eggs

You know what? I used to hate scrambled eggs when I was a kid – I think it's because my auntie Muriel always made that when we visited. Me and my sister were almost sick each time it was brought out. Psychologically we've been scarred. But, the good news about scrambled egg is that any twat can make it, so no matter how shit it tastes, it's worth making cos it's easy.

Actually, scrambled eggs have become one of my favourite things. And you *must* have this on 'working class' WHITE BREAD. Don't start going all middle class on me, bringing out a fancy ciabatta and pretending you're in Pret a Manger.

Ingredients

- 4 large eggs
- 6 tbsp of semi-skimmed milk. If you want to go all poncy, then you can use a bit of single cream or full cream milk
- A bit of butter – about as much as you'd put on a slice of toast.

Quick Q&A

Q: Can you do scrambled eggs in the microwave?
A: Absolutely, in fact, if you can't be arsed to clean out a frying pan after you've made it, then go for the easy option and bung it in the microwave. Keep opening it and stirring it or it'll turn out shit. Add some butter at the end to make it taste like your grandma made it whatever that means.

Scrambled eggs tastes good with:

- A nice cup of tea
- Some salt and pepper on
- Music to have on in the background: Shed Seven or The Cribs. I'd probably go for Shed Seven.
- Some people like ketchup on their scrambled eggs, but not me.

Some celebrities who probably like scrambled eggs include: Actor Tom Hanks, singer Emma Bunton and ex-leader of Pakistan Imran Khan.

Foodie tip
The key to good scrambled eggs is: make someone else make it.

Method

1. Lightly whisk 2 large eggs, 6 tbsp single cream or full cream milk and a pinch of salt together until the mixture has just one consistency. I don't use a whisk -why bother when a fork will do? And honestly, it's just as good.
2. Heat a small non-stick frying pan for a minute or so, then add a knob of butter and let it melt. As soon as the butter has melted, pour in the eggs/milk mixture. Let it sit, without stirring, for 20 seconds. Stir with a wooden spoon, and 'break it up' as it begins to set and scrape off the scrambled egg which begins to stick to the bottom of the pan.
3. Repeat until the eggs are softly set and are as moist as you like it. Remove from the heat and leave for a moment to finish cooking.
4. Give a final stir and serve the scrambled egg on top of your toast. DO NOT PLACE YOUR TOAST AT THE SIDE. That's the sort of thing they do in posh hotels. Tip your scrambled egg on top of your toast.
5. I was only joking earlier when I said you must use white sliced bread. Scrambled egg is great on sourdough bread or whatever you like. It's also great if you do some crispy bacon to go with it. This is one of my most popular meals. And it's also good if you have a few baked beans with it. You can just stick those in the microwave.

How To Boil An Egg

For fuck's sake, how difficult can it be? Well, for some, it would be easier to climb Everest while in a ballgown and wearing a pair of high heels. And the same goes for the women too.

What you need:

- An egg
- A pan
- Water

Step-by-step guide:

1. Put water in pan and boil it
2. Put Egg in water (while still in its shell, you moron)
3. Leave for five minutes.
4. Done

*For soft boiled eggs, leave in simmering water for about 4 minutes. If you take your eggs out too early you'll find that the bit around the yolk hasn't been cooked properly and it looks like a snot or frog-spawn.

Interesting Fact

Don't forget to peel the egg shell off the egg before consuming. I can't believe I'm even having to fucking say this, but I just have.

Don't dip your fingers into the water. Add salt and pepper to taste to the egg not the water!
For a bit of added nostalgia, make some 'soldiers' out of a slice of toast, and dip them in the yolk.

This page is dedicated to my grandad Eli, the man who invented the multiplex cinema. And when he died, we held services at 2.15, 4.15, 7.15 and 9.15.

How to Make a Nice Cup of Tea

You're probably thinking that anyone can make a cup of tea, but that's where you're wrong. There's a lot more to making a really good cup of tea than meets the eye. Of course, you can just bung any old tea bag into a cup, fill it with boiling water and then add some milk and that will be passable. But, do you want a LOVELY cup of tea you can enjoy and savour, or do you want a cup of tea that tastes like piss? I must point out that I have never, ever drunk a cup of piss, so I'm not an expert on urine but you know what I'm saying.

There are some golden rules you must follow when making a cuppa:

1. NEVER OUT MILK IN YOUR CUP FIRST
2. REMEMBER TO PUT A TEA BAG INTO YOUR CUP
3. ADD BOILING WATER AND LEAVE IT FOR A COUPLE OF MINUTES
4. REMOVE THE TEA BAG
5. THEN, AND ONLY THEN, ADD MILK!

Interesting Fact

Some people believe they can tell the future just by looking at tea leaves in the bottom of a cup after you've finished. Sounds like a scam to me.

1. Having a nice cup of tea on it's own is perfectly acceptable, but if you have it with a biscuit, it's even better. Here are my recommendations:
2. Tunnocks Marshmallow biscuits. They look like a little spaceship or something, and they're fucking fantastic.
3. Custard Creams. A classic biscuit. Beware: they are more addictive than crystal meth.
4. KitKats. A popular choice which never goes out of fashion.
5. Now, here's a controversial choice. Don't slag me off for going all middle-class, but I enjoy a little 'Madeline' treat with a cup of tea. For those who don't know what a madeleine is, they are like sponge cake in an individual wrapper, shaped like a miniature submarine. The main brand is called Bonne Maman which are really good, but you can also buy Tesco own-brand ones and they are just as good, only a lot cheaper. I like to pretend that I'm in a Paris street café when I'm eating mine, but you can pretend to be wherever you like.

Celebrities who I think love a cup of tea include...
The King of England (Charles)
Ed Sheeran
Comedy writer Richard Curtis
Boxer Tyson Furey.

How to make an omelette

You know, omelettes are strange things, they look like an alien life force or something. In fact, I remember an early episode of Star Trek that had 'omelette-like' creatures stuck to the walls and ceilings and then they would drop off onto unsuspecting people and stick to them. It was all very dramatic. If only the victims had thought about eating them, everything would've been alright. Anyway, I'm drifting away from the point here – how do you actually make one of the fuckers?

It's not very difficult to make an omelette. This is what you do.

Grate some cheese in advance (or get some cheese slices ready), plus anything else you want to stick in your omelette. Some bacon bits or pieces of sausage work really well in an omelette. Cook these in advance. Mushrooms are also lovely, so fry them first.

Omelettes are great with some chips, so don't forget to put some of those in the oven in advance… and you can also microwave some beans, because they go well with it too.

Quick Q & A

Q: How long does an omelette take to cook
A: I reckon about five minutes

Q: Is the word 'omelette' French?
A: I don't know. That's what Google's for, why are you asking me?

Q: If I don't want an omelette, can I make something else instead?
A: Yes, you can, thanks to Brexit!

Directions

1. Add a little bit of oil into a pan. I use vegetable oil. You could just use some real butter if you want to, it's up to you.
2. In a bowl, put 6 eggs, a little bit of milk and some salt and pepper. This omelette will make enough for two hungry people.

3. Pour this mixture into the frying pan…
4. Let the mixture settle and leave it. As it begins to take shape and cook, you can lift up the edges of the omelette and let the surplus liquid tip under it. This makes a nice, evenly cooked omelette.
5. Now drop in the grated cheese and anything else you want in your omelette. Some of you may be tempted to put in some healthy things such as peppers, but I think that is a shit idea.
6. Once your omelette is taking shape and looks to be cooked when you lift it at the edges, fold it over to it's now 'in half.'
7. After a minute or so, turn the whole thing over so it cooks evenly.

Tips

Why not make an omelette sandwich. I might even copyright that idea if I can. Add some Peri-Peri mayo to top it all off nicely.

Poached Eggs

If you've ever watched the TV programme 'Four in a Bed' where B&B owners go and critique other establishments, you'll know that in EVERY episode they go on about making 'perfect poached eggs' – they talk like it would easier to find the Holy Grail than making a poached egg with a nice, runny yolk. You DO NOT need thirty years of experience to produce a good poached egg. Jesus, for fuck's sake, it's just sticking an egg in some water. It is NOT difficult. The morons on that show shouldn't be running a B&B, they should be in straitjackets in the local asylum for the inept.

Quick Q & A

Q: Are poached eggs good for you?
A: Yes, they are very good for you according to popular online egg fan-groups.

Q: What happens if you cook your poached eggs for too long?
A: They become over-cooked

Fun Facts

1 Eggs have been used in many movies... although I can't think of any off-hand.
2 In America, a lot of people have their eggs 'over-easy' but no one really knows what that means...
3 Eggs are popular all over the world, and, if you can believe this – some people eat them raw!

This page is dedicated to my brother Clive who has spent most of his life in a wheelchair. He's not disabled or anything, just fucking lazy.

Directions

I'm going to tell you how to make perfect poached eggs every time. Any cretin can do it

1. Crack your egg into a bowl as this makes it easier to slide into the pan of water, and you can remove any bits of eggshell first. So far, so good!
2. Put some water into a pan – I usually put in about 4 inches of water. Don't put any salt in it because that breaks up the egg white.
3. Pour your egg into the simmering water. This means a few small bubbles, not a boiling tornado of water sloshing about that will break up your yolk from the egg-white.
4. Let it cook for about 3 minutes. You can see when the egg is about done, as it looks like you could 'pop' it with a fork. You can use a slotted spoon to gently lift the egg out so you can have a closer look at it. If it doesn't look done, pop it back in for another minute.
5. Lift out your poached egg and make sure all the water is drained off – or it'll make your toast soggy!

There, that's it.

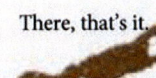

How to Fry Mushrooms!

How many of you wash your mushrooms before the bung 'em in to the frying pan? Yeah, I used to do that and then wonder why the pan was full of fucking water. The thing is, mushrooms are like sponges, so avoid washing them if you can. Or if they are really dirty, use a damp cloth and then dab them dry.

OK, so you now have some reasonably or very dry mushrooms. Slice them up how you like them. Put some oil into the frying pan. Not a massive amount, just enough to cover the bottom of the pan. Then place your mushrooms into the pan. Make sure they don't overlap each other. This is important, as if they overlap each other, they won't fry evenly.

The aim here is to get some nice brown and slighty crispy mushrooms. When you put the mushrooms in the pan – which should be on a medium temperature - LEAVE THEM AND DO NOT TURN THEM OVER FOR A COUPLE OF MINUTES.

When your mushrooms are a nice golden colour on both sides, add a little bit of salt and a blob of butter. That will finish the little buggers off nicely. And that's about it.

Quick Q & A

Q: Is it wise to go out and pick wild mushrooms and eat them?
A: No, unless you've got a death wish you absolute cretin.

Q: What do you do if you don't like mushrooms?
A: Don't eat them

Q: If I want to have, say, an egg with my mushrooms, is that OK?
A: Yes, as long as you have some eggs. If you don't have any eggs then I don't know what to suggest.

Don't be a prick and overload the pan with mushrooms like this!

Fun Fact

Mushrooms are the largest living thing on earth! Yes, there's a type of honey fungus which is 3.8km across the Blue Mountains in Oregon, USA. Most of this huge mushroom is actually underground and is responsible for killing trees in the area. That sounds like I've made it up, but I found this fact online, so it must be true.

The author (left) and his pals on his yacht having a mushroom party. And it looks like someone's stolen a button mushroom...

How to fry an egg

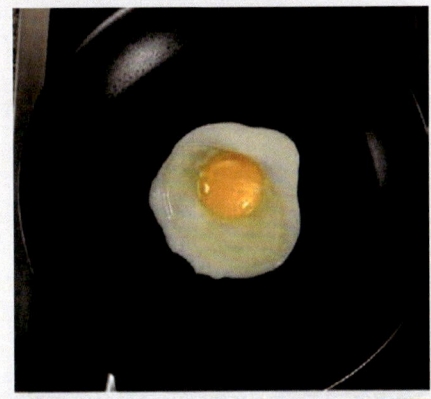

This is how to fry an egg so that when it's done, it doesn't have all that crinkly, burned bottom part. If that's the part you actually like, then I'll tell you how to do that at the end.

1. Firstly, pour some vegetable oil into a frying pan. Don't use olive oil, cos that's crap for frying an egg in.
2. Turn on the gas or hob on a low heat and then put your eggs straight in BEFORE the oil has got hot. This way, you get a nice even cook, with no burned bottom.
3. As the egg fries, scoop some of the oil in the pan over the top of the egg yolk to get a perfectly fried egg.
4. That's pretty much it. You can tell when the yolk is just right for you, by just keeping an eye on it.

*If you want the burnt crinkly bottom bit, then have the oil hot before you put your egg in, so that it crackles when it goes in. There, that wasn't so hard was it? Piece of piss.

Fried egg sandwich...

Use sliced white bread with some butter (or fake butter spread) on it.

Put your fried egg on top of one slice, add some salt and pepper possibly some ketchup, and then add a slice of bread on top. Then use a knife to cut the sandwich in half and you're all set.

This is great with crispy bacon or sausages added.

And don't forget a lovely cup of tea to go with it.

Did you know?

Eggs come in lots of different sizes – small, medium and large. And an ancient English by-law says that at least one egg in a box must have a tiny feather and a bit of shit sticking to it.

What do the experts say? - We don't know, as we haven't asked any.

QUICK AND EASY BREAKFAST

Nothing beats a good-old British breakfast. We love a plate full of grease with some stuff thrown in amongst it's what our arteries deserve.

A 'full English' as it's known, is revered around the world for its variety, its complexity and its culinary creativity. IS IT FUCK!! A full English is known for containing enough cholesterol to block even the most stubborn of arteries, all on one big, beautiful plate. It might not be the healthiest option, but it tastes so good that it's worth risking your life for.

Who can resist bacon and eggs, beans, fried bread, black pudding, sausages and hash browns all crammed together with a mug of hot tea? Absolutely no one, that's who.

But is it easy to cook? The answer is 'yes' and I'm going to give you a full English masterclass which I believe will give you a lifetime of cholesterol-related pleasure. But look, I'm not saying you should have a full English every day, have one twice a day! No, seriously, have one as a treat every now and again, and you'll love it. And as far as your heath goes, they're not half as bad as I'm making out, either.

The secret...

I don't think breakfasts are very difficult at all. The sausages, black pudding and bacon can be cooked in advance and then microwaved if required, and the beans can also be microwaved. The waffles are bunged into the toaster. This only leaves the eggs.

While you're frying the eggs, you just have to microwave and toast the other items.

Quick Q&A

Q: Does anyone ever eat their fried tomato on their full English?
A: No
Q: Can you have waffles and syrup on your full English?
A: Yes, in fact I recommend it.
Q: How many calories are in a full English?
A: According to online forums, it can vary, depending on what you cook.
Q: If you accidentally drop a sausage on the floor, is it still alright to eat?
A: It depends on how hungry you are, and if you are working class or not.
Q: What is black pudding?
A: No one really knows, but there are some scary stories online that suggest blood is involved. All I know is that they are really tasty on a full English.

A Pan

Professional TV chefs...are they all wankers?

Well, the answer to this is probably 'yes.'
But I must point out that I don't know any of them personally.

When I watch them on TV, they are so pretentious. They all want to make the simplest meals into some sort of complex masterpiece – adding things like fresh ginger and sesame oil. Basically, all the things that are expensive, and all the things you probably don't already have, so you have to go out and spend loads of money on fancy shit.

Does anyone really have any cumin in their cupboard? Thought not. And when they're sprinkling salt on food, do they really have to hold their hand over the food really high so that it looks really dramatic? Really? You don't need a Michelin Star to put salt on some chips.

TV chefs also tend to use the word 'drizzle' a lot. According to some working-class people I know, the word 'drizzle' should only be used in a sentence like this: "Is it raining? Well, there's a bit of drizzle…but later on it's going to fucking pour down."

Contestants on masterchef about to serve up a slice of cake to Greg Wallace...

Quick Q&A About TV Chefs

Q: I would like to be a famous TV chef and earn massive amounts of money. Do I need to have a gimmick like Nigella Lawson and keep dropping in double-entendres whilst she's having a drink?
A: Yes, it's always a good idea to have a stiff one.

Q: That chef who lives near the coast – what's his name, oh, that's it – Rick Stein. Does he always smell of fish?
A: According to ChatGPT, yes, he absolutely fucking wreaks of it.

Q: Sometimes when I'm watching MasterChef on TV, I'm secretly hoping that they burn something. Is that really horrible?
A: No, that is part of the fun. My uncle Kevin is actually a keen chef, and he's always burning things. Unfortunately, at the moment he's serving ten years for ar

A pan

Pan's can be very important in the kitchen as they are really good at holding stuff. Pasta is a typical example of what cooks nicely in a pan.

A toaster

These little machines are a fantastic invention if you just fancy some toast! My toaster is pretty shit though, as I sometimes have to cut a bit off one end of my bread or it won't fit in properly. Honestly, those toaster makers only have to consider one thing: "Can bread fit in?" And they can't even fucking do that!

A clawhammer

I don't know why I've put a clawhammer on this list, but I always think that it's useful to have one nearby should it be needed. I've never had to use mine yet, but it's there, all ready for that emergency situation.

Stuff you'll need.

Let's imagine that you've never ventured into the kitchen before, or if you have, it's been a fucking disaster. That may be because you did not have the right tools for the job, or it's possible you had the right tools, but not enough brain cells available to use them. Later in the book I will be talking you through a selection of utensils and what they are used for, but just to get things going, here are a few of the basic tools you will need to survive in the kitchen.

Microwave

My friend Louise says that the microwave oven is the best invention since the 'Rampant Rabbitt' whatever that is. Anyhow, if you've got a microwave, then you are well on the way to being as good as Gordon Ramsey. I must say that it's difficult to beat the thrill of making food using the harmless power of radiation. And even better, you can pick them up for around thirty quid in Asda.

All you have to remember is that you should NEVER put anything metallic inside it, such as spoons, tin foil or a NASA spacesuit. Oh, and don't put eggs in their shells inside either, as they will explode.

A scraper

Things are going to go wrong, so you might as well be prepared for that eventuality. A scraper will be invaluable for when you try and remove all the crap stuck to your walls and left in the bottom of metal trays.

A Drill

Sometimes, there will be left over food stuck to your pan or baking tray that will be almost impossible to remove. Thank god for Black and Decker!

Contents

Introduction. 6
Stuff you'll need 8
Professional TV chefs…are they all wankers? 10
QUICK AND EASY BREAKFAST............... 11
   How to fry an egg 12
   How to Fry Mushrooms!................................ 13
   Poached Eggs.. 14
   How to Make a Nice Cup of Tea 16
   How To Boil An Egg 17
   Scrambled Eggs 18
   TOAST 19
   Waffles 20
   Cereal - Why 21
   Your Kitchen Dilemma 22
   A Healthy Breakfast 23
Snacks and Sarnies 24
   A Greggs 25
   Banana Sandwich 26
   Beans on toast 27
   "It's a Wrap!".. 28
   Fish Finger Sandwich.................................... 29
   Crisp Sandwiches 30
   TOP TIP:... 31
   Microwave 'grilled' cheese sandwich.............. 32
   Hot Meatball Sandwich 33
   Cheesy chips 34
   Egg Mayo 35
   More Tools!... 36
   Peanut Butter Sandwich 38
   Hot Dogs.. 40
   The Perfect Cheese on Toast 41
   Kitchen Utensil Management......................... 42
HOW TO
   How to Cook Pasta.. 44
   How to cook rice 46
   How to keep things fresh............................... 47
   How to make your own Pesto 48
   Garlic Butter.. 50
   Garlic Mayo.. 51
   Salad. Is it any good?..................................... 52
   Which Oil?... 53
   Romantic Food 54
MAIN COURSES
   Burgers 57
   What the fuck is Asparagus?.......................... 58
   Tuna Pasta Bake 59
   Bangers & Mash.. 60
   Pizza Time... 62
   Piss-easy Carbonara 63
   Really Easy Spag Bol 64
   Dead Easy Macaroni Cheesy 65
   Chicken in Stilton Sauce 66
   Parmesan & Cream Cheese Pasta Sauce 67
   Easy Lasagne 68
   Smoked Mackerel & Rice.............................. 70
   Pesto Pasta with bacon and mushrooms 71
   How to make the world's best Yorkshire puddings... 72
   Vegetables: Are they *really* necessary? 73
   The Oven Chips Conundrum Explained......... 74
   The Perfect Chilli 76
   Having Guests Round?.................................. 77
   Gravy – what's that all about? 78
   How do you cook chicken?............................ 79
   Cauliflower Cheese 80
   Ultra-Quick Garlic Bread............................... 81
   How to do a Baked Potato 82
   Baked Camembert... 83
   Eggy Bread.. 84
   Fried Egg Sarnie.. 85
   Chip Butty... 86
   Pasty Butty.. 87
   Corned Beef Sandwich 88
   Cinnamon Butter Toast 89
   Crumpet Cheese & Bacon Toastie.................. 90
PUDDINGS & STUFF
   Bonkers for Blueberries................................. 92
   Biscuit Management 94
   Lemon & Blueberry Muffins.......................... 95
   Ice Cream Surprise! 96
   Rocky Road using Twix................................. 97
   Simpleton's Strawberry Cheesecake............... 98
   Easy Ice Cream Pudding 99
   Sticky Toffee Pudding 100
   Rocky Road with Biscoff!............................101
   Rice Pudding...102
   A Doddle of a Banana Cake.........................103
   Chocolate Cake for Dummies......................104
A final word from the author… 106
Credits 107

Introduction.

Hello.

For many people the preparation of food is an exciting, relaxing, and exhilarating adventure into the culinary world. We've all seen Masterchef on the telly and the wondrous dishes served up to the experts after an hour or two of intense cooking. Yes, those delicate presentations where a carrot is precariously but expertly balanced on top of lamb shank is an absolute wonder to behold… but we aren't all capable of that are we? Many of us struggle to open a bag of oven chips, let alone figure out how to actually cook them!

This book is a short cut for the inept, a helpline for the hopeless, a cookery book for the clueless and much more. Plus, I've included a selection of free swearwords in as a sort of crap bonus.

I will be guiding you through a whole host of recipes and procedures and even if you're thicker than the nearest pile of pig-shit, you will not starve. I'm taking you back to the basics, pre-stone-age and making things so simple that if you are the World Champion simpleton, you'll still be able to rustle up something that's almost edible.

I don't know about you, but I personally get pissed off with all those TV chefs concocting meals that will cost you fifty quid in ingredients by the time you're done. The recipes in this book are all very basic and as cheap as possible.

Look, you won't be winning any Michelin stars or anything else for that matter, but you will be winning at life!

OK, now let's get on with it, you must be feeling hungry by now…

Graham

COOKING FOR CRETINS

The New Bible for Kitchen Simpletons

By Graham Hey.

Copyright © Graham Hey 2024
Published: September 2024 by FCM Publishing
978-1-914529-97-9 - Paperback
978-1-914529-98-6 – Ebook

All rights reserved.

The right of Graham Hey to be identified as the author of this work has been asserted by him in accordance with sections 77 and 78 of the Copyright, Designs and Patents Act 1988. No part of this publication may be reproduced, stored in retrieval system, copied in any form or by any means, electronic, mechanical, photocopying, recording or otherwise transmitted without written permission from the publisher. You must not circulate this book in any format. Copyright of all imagery used within remains solely with their originator. No breach of copyright is implied or intended and all material is believed to be used with permission. Should you feel that your copyright has been impinged, please contact the publisher to ensure appropriate acknowledgment may be made.

Unauthorised reproduction of these recipes may result in extremely bland meals and a stern talking-to by your conscience. Remember, sharing is caring, but stealing is just plain tasteless.

Disclaimer: The publisher holds no responsibility for any injuries sustained, guests accidentally poisoned, or kitchens destroyed in the process of following these recipes. Cook at your own risk, and remember, a sense of humour is the most important ingredient in the kitchen!

Photography by Graham Hey